LOVE HOPED FOR

LOVE HOPED FOR

◆

A Memoir

Vivian Davis Campbell

iUniverse, Inc.
New York Lincoln Shanghai

LOVE HOPED FOR
A Memoir

iUniverse, Inc.

For information address:
iUniverse, Inc.
2021 Pine Lake Road, Suite 100
Lincoln, NE 68512
www.iuniverse.com

ISBN: 0-595-33407-5

Printed in the United States of America

Contents

Introduction

It has been my privilege to accompany the author, Vivian Campbell, through the last fifty years of her quest for love. She has been my wife, consort, friend, companion, and best mother of my life. I am pleased to have contributed in some small way to the triumphant end she describes in her Memoir.

The title was suggested to me when I reviewed her horoscope some twenty years ago when she first began to work on her book. She has the Moon in Cancer in the Eleventh House (Love Hoped For) conjunct Saturn and Pluto! Even a beginner in astrology would read that as a sure recipe for pain, sorrow, and frustration centering on her mother. Most of us would have missed the transformative experience indicated by Pluto.

The writing, itself, brought a kind of transformation, and the reader may find inspiration in it for pursuing their own quest for integration.

Charles I. Campbell
September 2004

Preface

This is the story of a loveless childhood and the lifelong search for love it engendered. The extent and nature of the damage to self from such a beginning is impossible to predict. As it extends into maturing years it can never be entirely mended. Only the most obvious consequences of such childhood wounding can even be recognized. For example the absence of affirmation in childhood may result in a paralysis of motivation in adulthood.

Much more has been learned about childhood influences than was available at the beginning of my life. But however much we have learned, to repair the past requires extraordinary efforts and gifted guidance. The meaning of many events in our lives is beyond knowing. Yet in spite of ignorance and appalling disasters, I survived, and I consider it a tremendous gift to be here and to be glad of it.

Without the patient help of my husband, Charles, I am not sure I would have been a survivor, and in any case there would have been no Memoir.

Vivian D. Campbell
September 29, 2004

My Father

From the very beginning of my existence on the planet my personality was defined and molded by my mother's declaration and attitude at her initial look at me as I was held up for her to see. "Take her away she's ugly." Her sister had a year before birthed what everyone thought an exceptionally pretty baby girl. When I grew into being an attractive pleasing young woman, actually better looking than my cousin the 'pretty baby girl Mother had to resort and reshuffle her initial conception of how to deal with the creature and its features she had not taken into account.

Now not yet out of bed from her confinement I'm sure she was reviewing her own youth and its problems as a female. Knowing her so well I have no doubt she was constructing and putting together the does and don'ts as she planned what activities she would allow me. She would make sure the dangers and hazards I might encounter would be avoided and disposed of by clear means and strict rules. Make them as ironclad as possible short of what she considered to be cramping and thwarting to a young females development and within the rules of socially acceptable behavior. This would give a sound structure for guiding and controlling me. This was not unusual with Mothers of that time. It had apparently not occurred or was generally not known to the arbiters of 19th Century society that such an agenda could have crippling and damage to a full and complete development of a child's talents and character. With Mother I believe she thought it would make it easier to manage a child she really didn't want. It worked more or less with me. I was told what to do and I did it. My curious and adventurous self only burst forth occasionally in breaking small rules. Outright rebellion or tantrum was not my way. What I thought of or didn't like were silent inside me. I had buried and forgotten a childhood of frustrated hopes for love and the disappointments that followed. Each little grave held the fragments of a painful experience: the dolls my father gave me, which my mother complained were too expensive; the sled, which brought the same complaint; my asking to sit on my father's lap denied because it would wrinkle the crease in his trousers. This was my preparation to venture forth into an unknown world, adult in years but an unprepared child in experience. I had never thought or questioned my motivation or even realized what my hunger was. Needy and yet fearful I plunged recklessly into a loveless marriage and found hope gone again. Crushed, I went back to home bringing with me my alcoholic husband too cruel and infantile to love anyone.

It was February in Ohio. Patches of old snow and ice filled the broken sidewalk slowing our progress. My father, Dr. Fred Davis, walked beside me, frail and shrunken from illness. I carried his old physician's bag. He was doing something he had done for as long as I could remember. He was making a house call. Barely out of bed from pneumonia—I wondered if he would make it down our street. Always reticent, now he said nothing. Alarms went off in me when I saw how weakened he was. He had always been a symbol of strength and determination, though he was remote and unreachable. I had seen him survive influenza, several heart attacks and now pneumonia. I realize now I had never given up hope that he would show some sign of his regard for me. I pushed down the fear and panic. Somehow I knew that losing him would be almost unbearable, and it was. This was his last house call. He died a few weeks later.

I know now that, undemonstrative as he was, my father loved me. He gave me presents, which my mother said were too expensive. He showered me with candy that probably ruined my digestion. I do not remember any words or hugs of approval from him. His distant manner and lack of outward show of affection gave the opposite impression to his only child. I had stopped trying to elicit it. I had seen him make a few attempts at showing affection to Mother. He tried putting his arms around her when she appeared in the kitchen in the morning only to be rebuffed or at most to receive an impatient shrug. Later he scarcely gave any sign of her arrival. With his death, all hope of eliciting some small sign of our kinship and his acceptance of me was abruptly extinguished.

My father never said anything of his relationship with his parents or his brother. I knew nothing of his feelings. How old was he when he realized that he wanted to become a doctor? How long had he planned for it before anyone knew of his ambition? As far as I know he had neither financial nor psychological support from his family. I never heard him speak of any friends. He had some cousins we used to visit who were warm and loving folks. In their company he was at ease and obviously enjoying himself. His family were Quakers, perhaps less judgmental and unforgiving than some other Christian sects, but austere in their habits and speech. Whatever emotion my grandfather felt came out when he sang old Welsh and Irish songs in his mellow and haunting tenor. At other times he was as reticent as my father. Working as a telegrapher, he earned an adequate living but with no frills and leaving little energy for warmth and affection. When my father communicated his wish to become a physician to his family, it so exceeded any ambition they had ever had for themselves or for him they were speechless. Not that they were not pleased and proud later on when he had successfully reached his goal. But at the time they were so astonished they couldn't speak of it.

Small and tough, Daddy managed to complete medical school while working 12 hours a day. He loved the practice of medicine, even with all its difficulties and hardships. It seemed to me that he was superbly equipped for what he did. He was painfully sensitive and intuitive with his patients. He also had an analytical mind capable of discerning subtle correlations. He was an acute observer of a person's bodily manifestations and movements. Whenever we went anywhere among groups of people, county fairs, regional or national exhibitions, or to the local lake to swim, he was always looking, looking, looking. Unusual physical characteristics or peculiarities he observed intently. As we walked along, whenever he saw something or someone that interested him, he would poke his elbow into my ribs and begin to tell me about this or that feature or characteristic of that individual and speculate about its origin. He noted things like skin color, bone formations, general posture and the way a person walked. He was especially interested in feet. He said one could tell something about a person's general health by the conformation of his feet and the way he put his weight on them. This constant observation of his and what he made of his observations must have seeped into my unconscious. In early adolescence and in my teens I noticed that I was looking and thinking too. If I had not been so emotionally crippled I could have made better use of it. Years later and after much professional and personal counseling, when I could use it more effectively, it was still there. When my husband and I first came to live in New York City in the early 60's I was so fascinated by situations and people I would begin to think about them and forget I was still staring. With persistence, Charles broke me of this by warning me over and over that I would attract elements to me I wouldn't want. I soon found this out on the subways where it's best not to focus on anyone. This process of looking, collecting facts and then thinking before acting has saved me from making a fool of myself in many critical situations.

Daddy had a number of serious illnesses, malaria, smallpox, influenza, anemia and several heart attacks. I like to think it gave him empathy for his patient's difficulties because he knew first hand the nature and symptoms of these diseases. Like other physicians of his time and place, he had to know and perform many treatments and procedures. He performed minor surgery, took out adenoids and tonsils, removed nasal polyps and other growths. He could set a broken leg, and he had done one appendectomy with the patient laid out on their dining room table. At the beginning of his practice the nearest hospital was in Toledo, and that was out of the question for most people. He had lost count of the number of babies he had delivered. A general practitioner of medicine, as medical practice was in the early part of this century; he was successful and highly regarded by his patients. The competent physicians also respected him among his colleagues. When he stood before a patient taking his pulse or his blood pressure or examining him otherwise, all of his attention was focused on that person at that moment. He was quiet, steady and relaxed unlike his usual high-strung, nervous movements. His hands never shook even in the last months of his life when his body was rapidly deteriorating. He took all kinds of cases, especially in the early part of his practice. There were no medical specialists in that rural area. Nor were there as many medical specialties in that time as there are now. Two physicians, father and son, who were acknowledged by physicians and lay people alike as the best qualified to consult in difficult cases, practiced in a town about fifteen miles from us. Father thought highly of them and sought their advice whenever he wanted another opinion. Most of the time he handled the difficult cases on his own.

One of these long-term and stubborn cases I can recollect quite clearly. The symptoms involved acute suffering and crisis whenever they occurred. The patient was an only child, a boy of nine or ten when he was first brought to the office. He had suffered severe seizures for about two years, and while the doctors could temporarily relieve the stress, the severity of the seizures didn't decrease. At the end of one of them the child would be exhausted and temporarily disoriented. I couldn't have been more than nine or ten myself the first time I saw him in one of these attacks, sitting there in his wheel chair teeth clenched, foaming at the mouth, quite helpless in the grip of this powerful and twisting force. They had rushed him to the office, but my father was out. There was little or nothing we could do. Mother coped as best she could by putting a knotted cloth between his teeth so he wouldn't bite his tongue. At the same time trying to keep the father calm. This boy must have remained a patient for fifteen years or more. At the time of his last visit shortly before my father's death, the attacks were hardly noticeable. He would turn pale, and feel a little ill. Knowing he was about to have a seizure, he would reach for his medication and soon be all right again.

Country doctors, then, along with all their other functions, were repositories of family secrets. In a household like ours where the office was at one end of our house we saw the coming and going of patients and their conditions. Inevitably their secrets spilled over into the family. I couldn't have been more than six or seven when I was firmly told that I was not to repeat what I heard at the dinner table, nor to tell anyone who did or did not visit the office. One of these secrets was that this little town of three hundred people had two or three drug addicts. They had become hooked on morphine when it had been prescribed as a pain-killer after dental work or minor surgery. They didn't come to my father for their regular fix. However once or twice a year something went wrong with their arrangements or their need for the drug. Then they would appear in the middle of the night at our front door, wild-eyed, face pressed against the glass, and begging for help. Sometimes Daddy would be out on a house call. Mother would turn on the downstairs hall light and we would peek around the upper landing to try to see who it was. Barely recognizing someone you saw almost every day in your trips around town, banging his fists on the door and begging you in a pitiful wail to give him a shot. It was a sobering experience for a seven-year-old. One of these individuals was the town barber. If anyone other than us knew his secret they never said. Just about everybody among the men and children got their hair-cuts and shaves there. Years later when I was applying for a job with the CIA, the FBI agent who was doing the security check for that area asked one of the locals if I talked very much. Could I keep a secret? He told me his reply had been: "If you asked that kid a question, especially if it was none of your business, she never knew anything. But you knew perfectly well by the twinkle in her eyes that she did know."

Every doctor has his share of nuisance patients. They're not in good health but they're also not very sick. But every little ache and pain and twitch scares them and they call or come to the doctor. Unless a doctor is experienced it is difficult to judge the seriousness of their complaints. Until he knows his patients quite well he must treat them all seriously. This often meant that the workload left little time for Mother and me. One time a patient called my father on the telephone in the middle of the night complaining he was in pain and couldn't sleep. He lived about ten miles from us. It was not much of a trip in warm weather even in the twenties in an open touring car with side curtains. But on this particular night it was winter and temperature near zero with about a foot of snow. In these conditions it was better not to make this trip alone. You might get stuck. Someone needed to maneuver the car while the other shoveled. It was almost always my mother who accompanied Dad on these night trips. They frequently alternated on the shoveling chore when they were really stuck, so one could get warm in the car while the other shoveled. Fortunately on this night they made the trip with only the normal amount of difficulty. As they pulled into the driveway they could see the patient sitting up in his easy chair reading the newspaper. My mother became a dragon in moments like this, so incensed that instead of words she would draw in her breath and give out short exclamations like 'well I never', or 'the nerve' or just 'well' followed by the forced exhalation of the rest of that breath. She would do this several times as if working up a good head of steam and venting her anger. But on this night she was too cold and too tired to do more than puff. My father was really angry but he held it, in the presence of the patient. When he came out he muttered, "That'll keep him busy for a few days." He had given the guy a huge laxative. It seemed to have worked for my father was never called there again in the middle of the night.

Daddy hated the telephone. If someone needed a doctor they rang the doorbell. In the beginning of his practice he had a telephone but he could never get a private line. We were on a party line with eighteen others. There was no AT&T then, only local companies. They were pretty independent about their service. If our ring sounded, everybody on the line picked up. They wanted to know who was sick. When this happened no one could hear anything. Finally one day there was a genuine emergency, and the party could not get through. After it was over, Daddy got in the automobile and drove to the county seat at Bryan, Ohio to the telephone offices and begged them to give him a private line. He went home and waited for about a week. There was no response. We had an old-fashioned wall phone made of oak with the black plastic mouthpiece and receiver. Since he still hadn't heard from them he was furious. He brought a crowbar from the basement, pried the telephone off the wall, and set it outside on the porch. After it sat there for several weeks the telephone man picked it up and carried it off without a word. Even though the service slowly improved after some years, my father never had another telephone. If someone needed him in the middle of the night they banged on our front door or got out in the driveway and cupping hands to mouth let out a yell that roused not only all of us but all the dogs in the neighborhood.

Daddy wouldn't give up on a patient until he had exhausted all his resources. He was not satisfied to just alleviate the symptoms in that phrase heard so much today "all you can do is". He didn't neglect the psychological aspects of illness either although he didn't segregate it from the other symptoms. He had a patient, in her early thirties who had tried to have a child. She would miscarry after several months of pregnancy. They desperately wanted a baby. The next time she became pregnant my father told her that she had a tumor but that it could not be removed until it had a chance to ripen. He told her not to worry if it became larger. At the proper time he would arrange to have it removed. Remember this was the late 20's and medical information did not circulate as freely as it does today. He carried her along like this for her entire term. When the labor pains began he sent word to her that he would come in a little while and that now the tumor could be removed. It was a fine baby boy and the only child they ever had. She of course had to take a lot of teasing from her relatives and friends. There was not even a diaper on hand for the new arrival.

Sometime in the mid-twenties father began to experiment with growing tumors in rabbits. I saw some of the large lumps on them but how he produced them I never knew. Later on he developed a plaster for removing surface growths. At one time he had a rather large number of these growths in jars in the rear of his office. It was a weird assortment of shapes, sizes and colors, growths he had removed from patients. One of my mother's sisters had a small lump on the side of her nose. My father told her he could take it out, without leaving a hole or a big scar. Early on the morning of the operation, Daddy went off in the direction of the railroad tracks about a quarter mile from our house. A sizeable ditch ran alongside the rail bed, which always had water in it, and always an assortment of small marine life, crawdads, minnows, water insects and frogs. Soon he returned carrying a brown paper bag and went directly into his office and to his compounding table. My aunt waited on the examining table. After a short time he came back and cut out the lump, leaving a hole of about half a centimeter in size. He placed a thin white piece of tissue over it and fixed it in place. I don't know how he made it stay there until it healed. After several months there was only a small scar and the skin over the hole was a little lighter in color. He had used the skin from the belly of the frog he had caught that morning in the ditch.

Up to then he had done a lot of work on surface growths. Then he got interested in what happened inside, particularly in the blood. He bought a microscope and started studying blood samples. He insisted that cancer cells were visible in the blood, a radical idea for that time. He examined microscopically several hundred blood samples. I was then entering my teens and not paying too much attention to what he was doing. A few years before he died he was working on a cancer remedy. It was a dye substance that he said if injected into the body would seek out and surround the cancer cells. The dye itself acted as a barrier to nourishment of these cells. Or, and I am not clear about this, the dye attracted radiation destructive to the cancer cells. The only verifiable evidence that I have is the following. Shortly after my father's death, his physician, a heart specialist, became interested in this work of my father's. We had a small male dog that had a growth on the exterior of its urethra. The cardiologist suggested that we take a sample of the tumor for analysis, and it turned out to be a carcinoma. As a test of the dye theory, we injected the growth and waited to see what would happen. Several months later the dog was still alive but very weak. We destroyed the animal and dissected the affected area. The tumor had not invaded the inner wall of the urethra. Because carcinomas are usually invasive, this is a small bit of evidence that the dye may have been effective in limiting the tumor's growth.

As I write this I'm both impressed by my father's ingenuity and embarrassed by his unorthodox and isolated way of working. Of what use was all of this effort? While he lived he helped a great many people, but if he had shared his work and his knowledge it might have helped many more. What was it that made him such a loner? One knows one's own pain all too well and how it isolates. Can we ever know the weight of another's? It may be so great that isolation from the give and take of one's fellows is necessarily almost total. Perhaps in some individuals productive work and investigation can only be done alone because the creative impulse is so delicately balanced that it cannot bear challenge while it is still being expressed.

Father was quick in his movements. I never saw him walk when he could run. He also had a hair trigger reaction to others' words or movements except with his patients with whom he was calm and steady. We were all, father, Mother and I, quick to react, and as a result there were almost no small issues in our family Stormy as it was at times, it was interesting. Some situation or event inevitably appeared which required action. Father got sucked into doing things for which he had no time or experience simply because he felt strongly they had to be set right. One of these was becoming mayor of our town. It was about the time that automobiles were being made that could be driven at a speed of 40 mph and with some cars a little more. Our town had two of the very few paved roads and they both ran through the center of it, one north and south and the other east and west. There were no state or local police. We had a town constable and the one sheriff for the county resided in Bryan. There was no one to patrol the roads and speeders (more than 25 miles an hour) created a danger when they went non-stop through town. Some of these offenders were young drivers from our area. A group of the more responsible citizens decided the town needed a mayor who could handle the problem, and they asked my father if he would take on the job. Today a town would probably petition the state government for a patrolmen or money to hire one. At that time no such thing was generally done. We made do with what we had, in this case the constable. He had an automobile, and so it was arranged that he would be paid out of town funds to function as traffic cop. He parked near the highway just beyond the crossing of the two roads, hidden from view by a store. There he would wait for the speeders and pursue them as they passed. This arrangement was a great success. He often apprehended five or six in a morning. We did have a town hall but my father was too busy to go down there and hear the cases. So they were tried in our living room. Evidence was taken, witnesses appeared, and the speeder was fined. He was not let go until he had paid up. This went on for about a month until my mother said it had to stop. It was interfering with our life and the use of the house, and it was also taking too much time from my father's practice. He enjoyed this role, for he had a great sense of justice, and he resigned rather reluctantly.

Daddy was not a good driver. Not because he couldn't have been, because his coordination was superb, but he just didn't give it his full attention. He would get to thinking about something and forget to look where he was going. He thought it a good idea for me to start learning to drive by first learning to steer. One day sitting on his lap and with some help from him, I was not doing too badly steering our Overland 70 on the straight stretch of road. However we came to the sharp left turn to get up to our street. That went all right in the beginning. My father pulled on the left side of the steering throwing into it the weight of his body, which was necessary with this automobile. Once he got me pointed in the right direction he went back to talking to his lodge brother and neighbor, Gary Fisher, who was sitting next to us. I could see that we were heading for a large maple tree on our neighbor's property. I couldn't get his attention. Gary also saw the problem and quickly grabbed the wheel and turned it back on to the road.

It was in this same Overland touring car with a canvas top and side curtains that Daddy had what could have been a fatal accident. It was summertime. My mother and I were weeding flowerbeds in front of the house. He had gone to make a house call in late morning and was now long overdue. Noon passed and then one o'clock and still no sign of him. My mother, knowing what a poor driver he was, began to fret. Then a car turned into our street, not the Overland, and slowly rolled up and into our driveway. I could see Gary Fisher sitting in the driver's seat and Daddy in the seat beside him. As soon as it stopped he got out, told Gary he was much obliged and at his usual pace started up the walk to the house. My mother, a little annoyed by this time, was about to speak when she saw that he was 'white as a sheet' as she later described it. Without a trace of anger she asked him if anything was wrong. He replied gruffly that nothing was the matter he had just been hit by a train. That's all. It was true. It turned out that a train had indeed hit him. He had not seen it coming and was already on the tracks when he did. The automobile's engine stalled before he could get out of the way. The locomotive engineer, seeing the car, slowed the train as much as he could. At the moment of impact the cowcatcher, as they called it, on the front of the locomotive caught the front fender of the Overland and carried it about a hundred feet down the tracks before the train, came to a full stop. The engineer got down from his cab and, when he recognized my father who had been his doctor, he nearly fainted. There was Daddy still sitting upright in the driver's seat, pale as a ghost, with his cigar clenched between his teeth. He was not hurt, not even a scratch, but the Overland was a mess. He must have been in his middle fifties at the time of this accident, still vigorous, doing his investigations, and seeing patients.

MY MOTHER

My father was aging. As he became even quieter and less active he became more dependent on my mother. She helped him in many ways. Driving for him, making his appointments for patients, and numerous errands, as well as the usual household duties. With Mother the changes were subtler. The heat had died out of some issues altogether. For others she reluctantly acknowledged that there were alternatives. When opinions were aired, she was just as outspoken as ever. But now her initial certainty was softened by the recognition that there existed differences that could neither be won nor adjudicated or for that matter even needed to be. Where one might have hoped there would be reflection and with it tranquility, there was only reluctant resignation, disappointment and fatigue. It was a combination of acceptance and denial, the old conflict without its former fire. The resignation showed itself in a kind of chronic fatigue. Her afternoon naps, one of her forms of escape, frequently lasted beyond the hour for preparing supper. She had more time for reflection and airing some of her regrets, probably the worst of which was her lack of education and recalling her very early painful childhood events.

She couldn't have been more than thirteen when she was compelled to quit school after the sixth grade, and hired out by her parents to work for other farm families. She was one of eight children in a family of Wesleyan Methodists. Mother's father was a farmer of one of those small, incredibly productive farms of one hundred to a hundred and fifty acres that exist, or did exist in two or three counties of northwestern Ohio. Much of the land was prehistoric river bottom soil, not only very fertile but also its products, corn, vegetables, and fruit had a superb flavor. I have never found produce of such goodness anywhere else, except perhaps in France.

All of the children, six girls and two boys shared almost equally in the work in the fields and barns. The girls also helped with the housework. This left little time for education or for fun. Too many loving words or gestures might lead you to sin. The Methodist idea, as my mother understood it, was that man was born in sin and doomed to hell unless he spent the rest of his life redeeming himself. To feel good about one's self was the work of the Devil and must be scoured from one's soul through self-denial and constant vigilance lest one fall in his snares. In practice it was something else. She once confided to me in a barely audible voice, that she had been forced by her parents, these same doctrinaire Methodists, to work and live with a man and his grown son in a household without women." Can you imagine what happened to me?" she asked, and began to weep. She simply couldn't be explicit about what must have been a sexual relationship with her employer and his son. What a tremendous conflict! Not even eighteen, with all the bloom and fire of youth, pitted against that "thou shalt not" conditioning. Speaking of it, she leaned forward in her chair, her head lowered. Part of her full of guilt and repentant, the rest dissolved in self-pity. I knew her so well after witnessing so many similar struggles in her. Here were the old adversaries at each other, rebellion and doubt. The former, the innate self, struggling for its existence, and the latter firmly established on its power base of guilt.

The contradiction between the doctrines her parents professed, and what they actually did was all too obvious to her. It turned my mother against as she called it "Organized Religion". Although she was a great reader of the Bible, she accepted only parts of it and rejected the Hellfire and Brimstone as she called it. Being a born pragmatist, my mother found the Immaculate Conception and the theory of vicarious redemption totally inconceivable. What she ended up with was a hodge-podge of valid religious ideas and pseudo-religious concepts. "Teachings" she called them. She had put together scraps and bits of ideas she gleaned from material appearing in tabloids whose circulation was predominately rural. She had answered many of these clever and convincing ads, which purported to have the truth about ancient philosophies. They were designed to convince the naive and unsuspecting reader, hungry for the 'truth'. These calls to salvation promised the way to fulfillment of all earthly desires, and even some of the heavenly ones would be found in their publications.

It is not clear whether there was more interest in religion then than now. For most people then the world was limited to their own backyard. Religious ideas offered them another dimension. Most of this material Mother read, thought about, and kept to herself. Years later when there was someone to share it with, she expressed her own edited and amalgamated version, and sometimes it was pretty weird. Mother followed one of these so-called religions, Spiritualism, seriously for two or three years. Surprising to everyone, my father also became interested. They must have felt that they had exhausted all the normal sources of affirmation, in addition to being miserably unhappy. They seemed to receive some kind of comfort from what they truly believed were communications from their dead relatives and friends. Apparently these same people who had been troublesome in life, now safely tucked away in another sphere, could be called to appear at your request. They were no longer the threat they had been in life. To make this contact, Mother and Daddy and I would go in the summer, to one of two or three spiritualist camps, usually located in rather remote areas in our part of Ohio, in southern Indiana, or New York State. Hundreds of other people had the same idea. There would be, especially on Sunday, two or three hundred at the lectures and message services. Séances were held where the dead supposedly talked. If you wanted to go to one of these it was ten dollars per person for the group ones, and twenty-five for a private séance. That was a lot of money for the early 1930's. For the spiritualist mediums it must have been rich pickings. Their clothes confirmed that they were doing pretty well, especially the lady mediums. Their fancy dresses were suitable for the most formal evening. The food and hotel people, generally relatives of the different mediums, cooked and served to packed dining rooms, for the two months the camps were open. The food, plain middle-western fare, was good. The mediums who went to these camps lived two or three hundred miles from us, too far away for frequent visits.

Then Mother found a woman who gave séances in Toledo, which was only fifty miles from our town. Every Saturday during the winter, we went to this woman for a séance. These were a real drag for me, in spite of the fact that we went to a movie afterward. Gradually Mother's interest waned after the Toledo woman died. It rather abruptly ended when my first husband smuggled an infra-red camera into a materialization séance. These were meetings held in a very dark room, where those who had passed on supposedly "materialized" so you could recognize them. Nothing appeared on the film. My mother's reaction to the camera was negative, but we heard no more from her about Spiritualism.

Mother had some strange ideas about the organization and functioning of the universe. I remember she once told my science-trained husband that no one could land on the Moon because it was a power station, and they would be burned to death. It reminds me of the story I heard about a Mullah in Pakistan, when he heard they were going to land on the moon. He warned them not to try it in the first quarter, because they would slip off. As for Mother, it's a pity for all of us who knew her, that she wasn't alive when they landed on that planet. We might have been treated to some astounding commentary from her curlicued conceptions. I never heard of her praying, nor did she ever mention God. She studied and worked at the spiritual exercises of the Rosicrucians for a little while. She was so secretive about it, however, that it was hard to judge it's worth. She did seem a little saner during that period. She spent a winter with us in New York in the early 60's. One day I found her talking to her image in the bathroom mirror. Patting herself gently on the cheeks, she was saying, "Now you've got to see me through to the end. Don't break down, you've got to get me through." I think she was addressing her remarks to her body. If so she had her wish fulfilled. At 88 she came home to Alvordton in May, from a winter with my sister in Detroit, went out into the garden on Monday and worked there all day every day through Friday. That night she began to feel ill, stayed in bed all day Saturday, lost consciousness Saturday night and died at noon on Sunday.

In her family, Sunday was the only day off. Close relatives living nearby gathered after church, at one house or another for Sunday dinner. At Mother's house the children usually went outside on a good day or up in the attic if it was cold or rainy and amused themselves after they finished doing the dinner dishes. Mother loved poetry, and she had learned and could recite a number of pieces, some classics and others sentimental ballads and songs. I'm not sure some of them didn't come from McGuffey's Reader. She was at her best reciting the sad and morbid ones. She brought to them the intonation and timing of the circuit-riding evangelists she had heard all her life. That and the full sepulchral tones from her German inheritance left few dry eyes. One Sunday afternoon when she was 12 or 13, she was standing on an old trunk in the attic with her siblings and cousins as audience, totally engrossed in her performance. Oblivious to the smallness of her stage, she stepped too close to the edge of the trunk, caught her foot on it and tumbled to the floor, hitting her nose on a nail. Her oldest sister wailed that she had attracted the devil. Holding her bloody nose, Mother lashed out that she had no fear of that entity, declaring that if the Devil came near, she would spit in his eye. She carried that attitude and the hump on her nose for the rest of her life.

Mother made a kind of life work of rebelling, or of trying to affect a change in her situation, either by outright demand or sulky retreat. She was often not able to accept her lot as it fell to her, even if it was tolerable by most standards. At best she found it distasteful, and at worst, unbearable. In the unbearable moments, if she could, she would go up to her bedroom and spend the whole day just lying in bed, sometimes crying, and generally feeling sorry for herself. When she emerged after one of these periods she was calm and quiet, and there was no trace of her recent torment. Rejecting just about all authority, except that which even she knew she had to obey. She was, as would be expected, especially hostile to religious dictums. She didn't just get this way out of her imagination. The rural clergy, Protestant and catholic alike, even up to my childhood, were narrow and bigoted, and for all I know, still are. A catholic priest, whose church was in Archibald, Ohio, a nearby town, used to drop in on us once or twice a year. He would lecture us for an hour or more, on what heathens we were, and at the end of his tirade, accept our dinner invitation and stuff himself on Mother's good food.

It's no wonder that Mother could not give up her suspicion of all doctrines and all clergy long enough to immerse herself in any one, either ethical or religious. She was totally unconscious of how thoroughly her values were fixed by her early training. They saturated her faculty of judgment and her behavior. My upbringing was a mixture of these same values and some quite contradictory ideas I was learning outside my home. I was conflicted by the difference between the facts of the time and my mother's absurd notions. Fortunately for me, in spite of the narrowness of her perspective, Mother believed in higher education, not as a mind developing process, which she knew little or nothing about. She thought of education as an economic liberator, an escape from manual labor, which she wanted most of all for and hoped that no child of hers would ever have to do.

Mother and her parents were largely ignorant of what knowledge there was and had all the superstitions and misconceptions that went with ignorance. It's difficult to conceive of this kind of ignorance if one has not witnessed it as I did, growing up in the midst of people whose education hardly extended beyond the eighth grade in second or third-rate schools. Libraries did not exist in ours or any of the towns nearby and as far as I know still don't. Most of the 'learning' they received after their regular school attendance was finished in summer Bible school or attending church on Sunday. In Alvordton, one had a choice between the Methodists and the United Brethren, a fundamentalist sect. Since Mother was so anti-Methodist, I went to the United Brethren Sunday School, until I disgraced myself one Sunday, when I asked where Darwin fit into the Creation.

It might have been possible for Mother to be emancipated from her early conditioning, if she had found a religion or ethical system that was compelling and attractive enough that she could follow it. Even if she had found a competent guide to help her it would have taken a multi-gifted genius to penetrate that protective shell of hers. Part of it was that she trusted almost no one. She kept most people at a distance. Real help would have had to appear at a moment, when by some miracle her defenses were momentarily inactive. This did not happen. One of the elements of this protectiveness was that she lacked humility. She bowed to no one, on earth or in Heaven. Although she was seemingly firm and in control, those who knew her well saw how she agonized over a decision, endlessly seeking verification.

Uncertain if what she had done was right, at the same time not able to acknowledge when it proved to be wrong. She fooled most people who thought her as impregnable as a battleship and as relatively free of problems. She saw herself as small and helpless, but to important issues she brought strength worthy of a Caesar.

Her parents forced her into an early marriage. My half-sister, LaVerne was born of that unhappy union, which ended when my sister was about four. This was about 1906 or 1907. Divorce was a real disgrace among Mother's people, so much so that forty years later, when I was about eleven, and discovered the certificate of her first marriage and the strange name on it, she, spoke of it in hushed tones, and of my sister being my half-sister. Difficult as it was to divorce, Mother managed it and endured the rebuffs and estrangements that followed. She was leaving the fears and uncertainties of her girlhood, and trying to turn away from her rigid and hypocritical upbringing, as she perceived it.

It is hard to realize how difficult it was then, for a woman to support herself, and with a small child. Her sisters provided food and lodging and some money. After several years of hard work and hard times, she began to make a reasonably good living as a fancy dressmaker. For the first time in her adult life, she was becoming truly independent. Then my sister developed a heart condition. With all the available treatment, her health didn't improve. The Doctor advised a change to a drier and healthier climate. Mother doing her duty to save her child, swallowed her painful memories and her pride and went to live with her parents in New Mexico.

Her father had lost his Ohio farm when a large shipment of hogs developed cholera and died, and he was unable to meet the mortgage payment. Having no other means of livelihood and very little cash, he did what many others had done in what is known as the panic of '93, 1893 that is. He applied for and received from the federal government, a homestead tract in New Mexico. He and my grandmother, with the help of their two sons, were trying to survive by farming this barren and treeless wasteland. A poorer economic situation would be hard to imagine. Housing was a sod shanty or a poorly constructed wooden shack. The dust seeped through the cracks whenever the wind blew. Apparently it blew a good part of the time and was strong enough that their youngest boy, my Uncle Hugh was able to experiment with wind sails on their old wagon. Water was scarce, and without it, land would not produce.

The life was acutely lonely for my grandmother. Homesteads might be miles apart and only a horse to get you over the distance between them. Whatever horses there were could not be spared for visiting. Recalling her loneliness, her eyes filling with tears, Grandmother confessed that she seldom saw or spoke with another woman from one month to the next. She was no crybaby. Grandmother was as tough as the leather in the soles of her shoes, which she used to alternately soak in water, and then with all her strength doggedly pound to softness, until the shoes were comfortable. She had lived through being a pampered child and then an orphan, bearing nine children of her own, one stillborn, suffering financial disaster, poverty and dust, and none of this had defeated her. But the loneliness almost deranged her. It couldn't have been much better for my mother, but she didn't express directly her dissatisfaction and psychic unease. Her unhappiness out there might have had its roots in many elements of the New Mexico environment. Mother hated dirt and bugs. What she generally would report if asked, was one or two or three trivial things out of the whole mass of her misery. For her this hellish time and place were dominated by tile dust and bedbugs. How she provided for herself and my sister, but she did. I'm sure it wasn't by giving poetry readings. But knowing Mother's resourcefulness, it could have been something as far out as that. Either she didn't want to talk about, or it was so disagreeable, or she felt it to be not quite respectable or even degrading. By the time I asked her about it, she couldn't produce a coherent picture for me.

Father, just out of medical school, came to New Mexico soon after Mother had come. His explanation had always been that he liked the West and wanted to practice there. But I like to think that he came because Mother was there. They had both lived in Toledo. Before leaving Mother had consulted a physician about my half-sister LaVerne's health, so that he knew where she was going. That physician could have been my father. If he was not, then this was all coincidence. In spite of all their personal difficulties, they must certainly have been meant for each other. The details of parents' lives, in fact their existence before they became one's parents, has little reality for children. Here may be a romantic tale, but it's almost impossible to think of one's parents as young and passionate.

It was difficult enough to begin a practice of medicine anywhere, but in the place my father had chosen it was impossible. This sparsely populated, poverty-stricken area lacked any redeeming element. All he had was his skill and knowledge of medicine and his dogged determination to try to make it work. It was not enough. He tried to make a success of it for perhaps two or three years. Whatever it was that decided them, they had to give up and go back to Ohio. Getting back was almost as difficult as trying to make it in New Mexico. They ran out of funds in Kansas City, Missouri. Daddy took a job in a pharmacy filling prescriptions. What a swallowing of pride this must have been! The three of them lived in one room, in a cheap boarding house. Mother must have worked, because by the time they left the West there was enough money to think about buying a property somewhere in the East. About 1913 they finally made it back to Toledo. Mother and LaVerne stayed with my mother's sister, while Daddy traveled around the state looking for a location in which to set up a practice. He chose a very small village, Alvordton, lying for half a mile along both sides of what later became U.S. Highway 20, in northwestern Ohio, about four miles from my mother's birthplace. The town had no physician. My father had no notion of its bad reputation. It was known as the toughest, meanest, little hamlet around. With a population of five or six hundred, it had six saloons, several bawdy houses, two churches, about five stores, and one livery stable. In the then recent past, men had been found dead in their buggies, under suspicious circumstances, just outside the town.

Two railroads converged at that point, the Wabash and the CCNY, and made a favorable place to establish factories and their related activities. It grew up in the late 1880's. At the height of its prosperity its population was about 800. It had never had a physician. When Daddy told Mother where he had chosen to live, she was horrified. In her teens she and her friends would visit relatives in that area. They were always warned to go around Alvordton, because it wasn't safe to go through it. If the choice was upsetting to Mother, what must her reaction have done to my father! He never revealed his feelings. I heard him tell someone once in a half-joking way, what the town was like then." You could get a drink or a woman", he explained, "but it was hard to find a good meal." It was no joke to

Mother even though her family treated it that way. It wasn't a momentary thing with her. She never quite got over having to live in Alvordton. She spoke of it periodically for years afterward, as if our presence there required an explanation. It was a terrible social comedown, just as she had moved upward through the professional status of her husband.

Whatever Mother's reaction, it didn't stop Daddy from working his head off to get a practice going, and it didn't take him long to do it. Within a few months the driveway was full of patients. He was reaping the rewards of being the only doctor in the immediate area, and of being a conscientious practitioner, even though it meant an eighteen hour day and house-calls besides. At last he was doing what he had long wanted to. In spite of the uproar and unpleasantness over father's choice of location, Mother's streak of good sense ultimately prevailed. She just put aside all the objections she had had, and began to do her part to establish a home and a practice. As they went over requirements and plans for living and working, Mother soon discovered how little Daddy knew about anything outside of medicine. Fortunately he knew it also, and was more than willing to leave the execution of the work to her.

Even when Mother couldn't actually do some part of the work herself, she knew the area so well that she could find someone who could. She loved organizing work projects, and keeping an eye on their progress. She hadn't had any training for this, but she had a very active visualizing faculty. She could see the steps in the process of completing a job, and knew what it should look like in detail and fit. For example she had watched her relatives at work in carpentry and had discerned that there was a certain logic related to the way structures small or large were put together. With this knowledge and her eye for soundness, they bought a property with two houses. They got the sheriff to oust a family of thieves in the smaller one, which they lived in while the large one was being remodeled. One of Mother's many cousins and his helpers did the work. Being German made it pretty difficult for them to take orders from a woman even from their cousin. At first they went to my father with questions, but soon found out that Daddy couldn't give answers, and didn't have time anyway. Grudgingly, they finally accepted my mother's advice and help.

The work was finished in late 1914 or early 1915. They spent part of September 1915 with my father's parents at Lake Erie. My mother, seven months pregnant, was such a clever dressmaker, that his folks never guessed they were about to become grandparents. I was born on Thanksgiving eve at 11:10 p.m. I know the birth time, because my father was meticulous about such details. Mother had cleaned the turkey for the next day's dinner, even though the pains had started. It was a difficult birth. My father had his hands full trying to get a birth cry out of me, and then trying to stop my mother's hemorrhaging. He succeeded in both, fortunately. My Aunt had had a beautiful baby girl some months before, and I think my mother was hoping I would look just as beautiful, if not better. I was a disappointment. When my sister proudly held me up for her inspection, Mother took one look, I am told, and said, "Take her away she's homely!" If a baby is sound what difference is it what it looks like? They are so cuddly and besides their looks at birth is not much indication of what they will look like as adults.

My half sister LaVerne, aged thirteen, delighted to have a baby sister, accepted me with open arms, and played with me much as she would have a doll. To me it was loving attention and I took all I could get, including being picked up when I fell. My mother's initial reaction to me didn't stop her from functioning as a good Mother according to her Methodist conscience. This impelled her to give me care and attention, even if I had looked like a baby ape. She would have felt she was shirking her duty not to. But I never remember a wholehearted response of acceptance as when one takes a child in one's arms, and loves them uncondi-tionally, because they are they, and so loveable.

Such a wholehearted positive response was almost impossible for my mother. Part of her attention was always caught and held by some dispute between con-flicting needs, of which there never seemed to be a resolution. Her still active hope for love and affirmation, and her long history of disappointment, restrained her reactions. She could not give unconditionally because she was still waiting to receive. This conflict didn't show in what she said and the way she said it, unless you knew her well, or were naturally perceptive. Someone who took account of the way in which a person presented himself, but didn't know that person well, would have said on meeting Mother that she was very reserved. She was that. Something was always held back. She did not give the appearance of being timid in expressing herself. She would throw back her head, straighten her shoulders and emphatically declare her opinion. But what she was expressing was always reinforced by the fear that she wouldn't be heard or listened to. I don't believe she was ever directly in touch with that fear, such as being aware of her heart beating faster or heightened tension. She appeared to most people to be generally calm, confident and full of strength. Sometimes she would hesitate for just an instant before replying. Given a concrete situation with no emotional overtones, whose elements she could readily judge, she showed remarkable strength and courage.

These qualities were clearly demonstrated in an event which occurred years before my birth. She agreed to accompany her older sister on a Great Lakes trip on a freighter with the sister's husband, who was the Captain. They had a very pleasant and uneventful trip to Lake Superior from Toledo, had unloaded the cargo and were ready to make the return voyage. It was late November, a stormy night, high winds and freezing rain, when they prepared to sail. The Captain, Mother's brother-in-law, in agony with an abscessed tooth, had rounded up the crew, too drunk to man the ship. Mother's sister, his wife was of no help in this situation except to moan that they were all going to drown. This was the same sister who had years before, cried out about the devil, when Mother fell off the trunk in their attic. She was not made of the stuff to attempt to navigate a large ship under those conditions. My mother was. She volunteered to steer the ship. Rain freezing on her face and reassured from time to time by the appearance at the door of the helm-house her ailing brother-in-law, she made it through a very rough night, without accident to her or to the ship.

Such strength is even more remarkable when one knows how little self-confidence she had. But she had a plentiful supply of will, determination, and just plain grit. The ship was her adversary and she would conquer it. However in most life situations we're not required to rise to such a challenge. Perhaps Mother would have been happier with a life which more often challenged her character and constitution. By way of compensation she sometimes made too much of an incident or of something my father or I had done. She dramatized it far beyond its importance. I suppose it provided excitement for her and exercised her dramatic talents. But Daddy and I came to resent its overcharged quality and her general unpleasantness. There was often an element of *j'accuse* in it. Mother was superb at putting this energy to work steering ships through storms, but the force she used to steer our household was excessive and left us resentful and exhausted. Ordinarily and in her calm times Mother was competent, good at all the home-making arts, She said of herself that she was a 'jackass of all trades and master of none.' But this wasn't true. She was a superb cook, gardener, and seamstress. She occasionally spoke in public, and for several years held the chair of Worthy Matron in her Eastern Star Lodge. She coped daily with the problems of having on her doorstep a large number of sick people and their often unreasonable needs and demands. Year after year, we enjoyed the produce and beauty from her garden. She made beautiful clothes for my sister and me and for herself. She even made my father's shirts when he complained that the collars on store shirts did not fit him. She was a source of strength and counsel to her neighbors and relatives, and the few friends she had. She could expertly bandage wounds, and she knew the antidotes to several substances used in prescriptions which if swallowed could cause death. I remember the neighbor next door rushing over to say that her grandson had swallowed the tablets my father had prescribed for her. My mother knew at once what to do, and beating up an egg white she forced it down this six-year-old's throat. In a short time he threw up a quantity of tablets. Mother was working overtime to be loved and needed without ever knowing the reason.

While I was still in high school I realized that my mother was insane—perhaps only temporarily I hoped. She would accuse my father and me of plotting to have her put away, or that he was secretly giving me money, or some other equally preposterous idea. I suspect that somewhere in her she knew that she probably should be put away. Thinking over her words, actions and behavior and talking to my father—for once we had a good talk—I decided that in addition to her extreme anxiety she was in menopause. He agreed. Being current on all the medical literature he received, I suggested she have estrogen. He thought it was a good idea, but he wouldn't give it to her. I volunteered if he would show me how. It was a messy business. The stuff came in peanut oil in those days, and it was difficult to get it into the body. It did help her, and seeing that, my father continued the shots after I went to college.

While her anxiety was as extreme at this time as I had ever seen it, it was never really absent, except when something would tickle her, amuse her and she would giggle wholeheartedly over it. There was a period when Mother fell downstairs several times. I think it was because she was in a hurry and didn't watch her step. She would go rolling down the stairs, end up at the bottom in a half curled up position. She never seemed to be hurt and she always found it hilariously funny. One time she came down with the alarm clock, it slipped out of her hand and bumping along, set off its alarm. This brought my father in from the kitchen. She would, still giggling say "unwind me slowly I'm not hurt." My father would remonstrate with her that" she would kill herself one of these days." One of the few signs that he still cared for her.

Mother took to spending a great deal of time at her dressing table in the morning. Sitting before the mirror she would make up her face, carefully comb and put up her long hair. Then spend several more minutes looking over the results and poking and pushing the hairs into place. I can't remember whether she devoted so much time to this when I was growing up. It seems unlikely that she had the time. Anyway she spent so much time at it that my father had to wait for his breakfast. Not being a patient man he took to getting his own and hers as well.

I realize now that the relationship had begun to come apart years before when I was still in grade school. There were always quarrels over money. Either there was not enough or one or both of them misspent it. Infrequently, but too often for comfort, my father would come out of his office, and find my mother standing there, he would go up behind her and kick and shove her around. I was horrified. How could anything be so violent that started from seemingly nothing? Long after his death and shortly before hers Mother told me that their sexual relationship was totally unsatisfactory to her. Now I know he was the husband spurned. Passing into the kitchen one day I beheld my father embracing the cook. I was so upset I ran screaming to my mother who was upstairs. What ensued I don't remember. I have blocked it out and can't recall it. I remember she did lock him out of the house once and he stayed with the Fishers for two nights. His frustration must have been extreme. It apparently disturbed his reason to the point of vengeance. When he died he left her nothing except a few dollars owed to him by patients.

Although their relationship was never anywhere near ideal it was far better when they were younger. My older cousin told me about the summers she spent at our house when I was still a baby. She said it was a cheerful and interesting household. My father had patiently helped her when she cried because she could not get the sewing right on a doll's dress she was making. They had fresh raspberries for breakfast, homemade pies, and beautiful flowers on the table for every meal. There was a coming and going of relatives and friends, holiday dinners, and evenings at lodge events. My mother was 36 and my father 46 when I was born. This account of my cousin's was certainly of happier years than I had generally known.

It seems to me incredible that two people with as much ability as these two had that they didn't have enough sense to work over their differences together.

However it was the time when investigations into a person's psychology were just beginning to filter down to the day-to-day medical practitioners. The emotional fatigue on both of them must have been enormous. It was so close to the surface that it would burst forth sometimes at the slightest provocation or no provocation. Arguments, angry outbursts, violent verbal exchanges happen in many families, but they are balanced by loving gestures and acts. It is so obvious to me now how starved they must have been for emotional support and neither could give it to the other. Neither had been loved or affirmed, nor had they any example of it in their families. The idea of giving one's self, doing for another without any wish for reward was inconceivable and impossible for either of them. They would have considered it close to prostitution. When their hope for love died, vengeance both subtle and overt took over. My mother withheld her favors and my father physically punished her for it. I suspect what kept them together was their unacknowledged need. They were so dependent on each other for the basic needs of life and had accommodated themselves to the miserable status quo the idea of separation had never occurred to them.

MY SISTER

When I think of my sister, warm feelings from early memories of her float up together with an incredible mixture of negative feelings, sorrow, resentment, pity, dismay, and anger. I can hardly believe that her words and her actions after I had become an adult came from that loving person I knew as a baby and young child. We got along famously then. It was when I began to have thoughts and ideas of my own, that she often didn't approve of me and said so in her vinegary tone and language. I never saw in her signs of striving for love or approval, except an occasional gift presented without comment. Control was her bag. Social work was her profession. The reports that have floated back to me say that she was a demanding and difficult supervisor as Head of AOC in Wayne county Michigan. Her early childhood, from what I know of it, wasn't exactly preparation for the emergence of an agreeable and generous adult. While my mother was trying to make a living for both of them with her dressmaking, my sister must have had to find her own ways of filling her time and of surviving emotionally.

I remember a particularly poignant story, which my mother in her almost total insensitivity, would tell over and over again in my sister's presence. When Mother and my sister were first living in Toledo and my sister was in early grade school, she took to regularly running away from home. She would go to an entirely different neighborhood where a special school friend of hers, a little Polish girl, lived. After she had done this several times in the same week, my mother knew she would have to take some corrective action. It would sometimes be dark before sister was found. When she went to give her a bath one evening, Mother discovered that she had head lice. This was out of the question for any child of hers. Mother wasted no time in finding an effective way to stop the running away. Being poor, her resources for a solution were limited. There was a convent near where they lived. As soon as she could she went to see the Mother Superior about putting my sister there. The arrangement would be that my sister would live there, and Mother would visit her as often as she could. She would not be allowed to go out without an escort. Whether my mother ever really would have done this I don't know, but she succeeded in convincing my sister that she meant it. When my sister was told the plan, she cried and cried and begged not to have to go there. "All right," my mother said. "If you promise never to leave me again, I won't do it." My sister agreed, and she never did leave my mother. Years later, Mother raised some objection to a young man whom my sister wanted very much to marry. He had been the school principal at our school. He was very good looking, agreeable and intelligent fellow. We all liked him, including my mother until she found out they wanted to get married. Mother objected to him on some petty ground, but enough so that my sister didn't marry him. While she worked in different cities at different times in her life, she seldom let more than a month go by without going to see my mother. She wrote to her faithfully every week, or called her on the telephone. Mother lived with her the last year of her life. Less than a month after Mother's death, sister's health began to fail. The cancer she had had eighteen years before, recurred and four months later she was dead.

In my infancy and early childhood, my sister was a second mother. She was almost too attentive. If I fell down she picked me up. She rocked me and fed me and sang to me. When I was five years old, beginning my first year of school, she went away to college. I don't remember any great trauma at the moment of her going. Perhaps someone, to ease the parting, told me it wouldn't be long, and she would be home to visit. With some events there is no loud signal to indicate its critical nature. It is only later that another event reveals its importance. When she came home for her first holiday from college, something happened which showed how much I had missed her, and how important she had been in my life. Even now, every detail of it is as clear as when it happened. Everything is there except the pain. We met her train in a nearby town where a close friend of my mother's lived. We stopped to call on this old woman. She was sick and needed someone to be with her. My sister volunteered to stay the night with her. When I comprehended what was about to happen, and that "sisto" as I sometimes called her, wouldn't be going on to our home with us, I set up such a howling that everyone stopped talking. No one including my sister could understand what was wrong with me. They made a feeble attempt to find out what I wanted. I was too young and too upset to tell them. One is often not aware of the critical moment of severance in close relationships. Perhaps that evening marks the end of my almost infantile dependence on her.

She was home less and less. My time was taken up with school and the children who became my playmates. Later on when I was ruining my meals and my figure with too much candy, I remember her chasing me across the yard, and me wriggling under the fence between our house and the schoolhouse so she couldn't take the O'Henry bar away from me. She had some peculiar and old-fashioned ideas. When Kleenex first appeared she thought it was unladylike stuff. A hand-kerchief was the proper article to blow one's nose into. At the beginning of WW II, when ladies boots were beginning to replace shoes and galoshes in the winter, she thought them too masculine, and ugly, and ridiculed me for wearing them. I lived with her in Cleveland during my first year at Art School there. I wanted to attend a concert of one of my favorite singers, Lanny Ross, at the municipal audi-torium. She laughed at me for wanting to go, but she finally agreed to accompany me. When Ross walked onto the stage and up to the microphone he tripped over the cord. She teased me for a week about his awkwardness, never once praising a performance I enjoyed immensely. It was as if everything I did, or had anything to do with, ought to be without flaw. I was glad when she took a job in Detroit even though it meant giving up a nice apartment.

Actually we never talked intimately about our feelings and aspirations. I don't know what her personal life was like in the years when she was still young and away from the rest of the family. I know of only one romance. She talked about it at the time without saying anything really enlightening, except I could tell by her expression and the tone of her voice, that she was very fond of him. This was about 1930, and after several years in Detroit working as an engineer, he had gone back to Italy. While we were living together in Cleveland she expressed an interest in inviting as she called him "an old flame", the man who earlier had asked her to marry him, to dinner with his wife. Whether she was trying to prove to herself that it was dead, or to see whether her judgment had been bad, I never knew. Whatever her reasons, they accepted the invitation. Young as I was, I thought it was a dreadful evening, and now wonder if it wasn't pretty tortured for her. Her reaction was to laugh about it. It was a mystery, like so many other things about her. Why did she respond with laughter, at some of the most seri-ous, distressing, and sad moments of hers and others' lives?

At the beginning of World War II after my father's death and my divorce from my first husband, I went to live with her again, so I could finish college at Wayne University. She agreed to feed and house me. It was an offer she couldn't sustain. At the end of the first semester at the University, she told me she couldn't continue the arrangement because it was using up too much of her income. She urged me to get a job. I was not qualified to do much of anything, and had to take a really puny job at the J.L. Hudson Company, filing invoices, for eighteen dollars a week. I was fed up at the end of two weeks. Fortunately it was early 1942 and the government was hiring. My first real job, with an annual salary of $1200 per year, was with the then War Department's, Tank-Automotive Center. With almost no income tax to pay, I was rich. This was the beginning of my war experience and series of rapid advancements. There were so many jobs and not enough people to fill them. From then on until 1945 it was work with little social relief.

On my twenty-ninth birthday, sitting at the breakfast table, it came over me that my life was passing and I hadn't had much fun and didn't see much prospect ahead for it. "Here I am 29 and nothing has happened to me," I said, crying into my cereal. "I thought life would be more interesting. I haven't found anybody to love and nobody loves me." By this time I was sobbing. My sister found this very funny. Although she was already in her mid-forties and nothing much had happened to her, she didn't seem to realize that or to care. This was 1944. Soon after this she moved to Flint Michigan and out of my orbit pretty much forever except for brief exchanges, which often included critical comments on my personal qualities. One of the first things she told my new husband was that I never finished anything I started. When early in our marriage we were trying to adopt a baby, she declared to me that she didn't think I was fit to be a parent. I was too stunned to ask her what made her say this. I was not so knowledgeable then about myself, and it cut deeply. After a few of these attacks, I limited my remarks to her to the most superficial matters. She had a habit of stretching and groaning and moaning. Sometimes she would be sitting quietly and suddenly let out a great audible sigh. No one could have been more surprised than I was on reading her farewell letter to me in which she said: "I have always loved you and I always will" and that she was leaving me all her earthly possessions. She is more of a mystery than anyone I have ever known, but I thought her life was about as dull as any I could imagine.

My Childhood

For my first thirty years I was almost totally unaware of what motivated and moved me to act in major decisions. My reasons and the feelings connecting them were hidden to me. Unconscious of my struggle, I was trying to put together a person that would be loveable. I had buried deeply within me a childhood of frustrated hopes for love and the disappointment that followed. Around age four or five hearing my parents argue, I felt bad. Terror in the night, angry voices, my father accusing my mother, "You did not want my child." What-no one wanted me or only my father wanted me? Was something wrong with me? What had I done? The source long forgotten, yet years afterward I would awaken in the night feeling sad and lonely. Only later did it cease to trouble me when with professional help I brought the source of this sadness into consciousness. Later events showed that my father wanted me more than my mother did. Even now I'm not sure whether I was more of a pleasure or a bother to her. She was very proud of my adult accomplishments and urged me on to greater efforts. But I see this was not love. When she pushed me to achieve, and the incessant dos and don'ts became intolerable I turned on her with my pent-up resentment and sense of injury. I told her what I thought of her as a mother. Then she whined that I didn't understand her or what she was trying to do. It was part of her game to hide in this "it's your fault that I am this way." Until I began to see through this she could make me feel it would have been better that I had not been born.

Although I was younger than the other children in my grade, almost from the beginning I was the leader and deviser of our games. I had heard just enough fairy tales to think up and organize imaginary expeditions and quests. I was also able to persuade the children to help and to participate. Our house was next door to the schoolhouse and if at noon hour or recess I thought we needed some item to make the game more real, I would send one of my playmates to ask my mother for it. They were quite willing to run these errands. I had no protest or opposition from them until one day my mother called the little group of my playmates over to the fence between our home and the schoolhouse. She instructed them not to run any more errands for me. "Let her go for them herself," she said. That day my little world fell apart. Mother would favor them against me? It's impossible to describe the humiliation and stabbing defeat a six year old can feel when abandoned by its principal support. Self-esteem rapidly vanishes. If we are fortunate recovery is possible bit by bit in time with a great deal of expert help. I do not believe that one's ego intact ever returns to its former condition. Fragments of it remain and continue to function in a patched up equilibrium. The organism almost at once strives to restore itself. It will attempt to mend the injury, alleviate the shock, and find new pathways and new modes of expression. Some traumas remain with us throughout life. I must have gathered myself together, somewhat agreeing with my mother that perhaps what I had been doing wasn't right.

I didn't give up the idea that if I could find the right thing that would please Mother she would love me. From her, the signals were mixed. I don't ever remember any real praise. Acknowledgement, but there were always "yes buts" and "why didn't", and "you should have" to go with it. Mother, Victorian and Methodist that she was, thought that this was the proper course of action so that I would not get an inflated opinion of myself. She said to the children, "You're spoiling her."

Children aren't fools. They are often cruel and devoid of mercy until they have been taught it. They picked up on my mother's message at once. Their attitude and acceptance of me was reversed. "She can't tell us what to do." Once such an attitude gets going it spreads and becomes a habit. I still played with them but was constantly reminded that I couldn't have any say in what they did. This new attitude of theirs over time spread to just about every element in our lives. This all took place in this same little village my father had selected and my mother had not liked. Now there were only about 400 persons living there and the railroads had nearly stopped running. Life was harder and poorer than ever for most of them. The Switchman in the tower by the railroad station was the highest paid inhabitant. Most of the dwellings were substandard wooden structures, heated by one pot-bellied stove in the center of the house. They were all firetraps. Probably the simplicity of the occupants' lives and the Mercy of God kept them from going up in smoke. Several houses, which while by no means luxurious, met the standards of good construction. One was the banker's, another the Schoolteacher's who had inherited hers, and ours. We had a coal furnace, which never seemed to work. We did have hardwood oak floors and plaster walls and a kerosene stove for cooking. On washday, someone had to turn the handle of the washer, white clothes had to be boiled prior to washing, and difficult dirt rubbed out on a washboard. Lacquered nails would never have survived this routine. We had a series of 'hired girls', young women from the farms around us, wanting to make some extra money before they married.

When the children I played with were old enough, they noticed the differences in the way our family lived from the way they lived, even though the difference was small. In any occasion of dispute I was reminded that I thought I was better than they were. How can a child refute such an idea? It had never occurred to me even to think about it. They undoubtedly heard this from their parents. I seemed to rebound from these assaults and went on with my childhood. I never remember challenging their idea of me or defending myself. My parents had the attitude of 'do and never say die' and eventually you'll get what you want. It was a kind of counterbalance for their limited value system. Without any doubt, I incorporated this into my *modus operandi*. For a long time it was my principal mover. It worked well enough to get me through a good many trials and failures, and the underlying optimism of it sustained me. Ultimately it had served me well and helped me to find the love I had always hoped for.

Christmases and birthdays were difficult times. Unable to show affection directly, my father bought me expensive presents for these occasions. My mother generally contested these purchases saying they were too expensive. My first memory of this was a large handsome doll with straight hair and bangs like mine. He had gone all the way to Toledo to obtain it. I received it with delight and hugged it to me. Almost at once my mother started to upbraid him for getting it for me, saying it was too expensive, it would spoil me. One of their arguments ensued. I remember gently placing the doll in the corner under the Christmas tree and going out of the room. I don't ever remember owning any other dolls.

Another Christmas I had asked for a sled. I was seven or eight or nine. I had in mind a sled about the same height as I was when upended. Father bought me a large sled, something I suspect he had calculated I would grow into, and therefore be able to use longer. There was what seemed to me a terrible row over this. My mother argued it was too large and too heavy for me. I would hurt myself with it. My father insisted to her no matter what he bought for me she would make a fuss about it, which was true. No wonder he showed less interest in us as time went by. Anyway I remember feeling sad but also wanting to try out the sled. There was a lot of snow on the ground, and had been for several weeks. It would be well packed down on the hill back of our house, and good for sliding. I went outside, well bundled up, and over to the top of the hill. I felt so bad I couldn't bring myself to slide down. I just stood there stiff with sadness and cold, wondering what to do. More than forty years later, when I saw the film Citizen Kane, I experienced a flashback of that winter day. I wept and wept as I sat in the darkness of the theater.

The children in my town didn't get any kinder as they got older. A year or so later I took this same sled to the nearby pond to 'belly flop' with the other children. As I slowed down from my first glide, one of the older boys, he was about sixteen, grabbed my sled from under me, threw it on me and jumped on it. Pounded as I was, I picked myself up and borrowing from my father's small but choice stock of profanity, I cursed this rotten kid for several minutes with all the words I knew and tearfully made my way home. When I tried to explain to my mother what had happened they just couldn't believe that anyone could be so mean. Whenever there was some trauma involving other children my mother always asked what had I done. I must have done something to provoke this. I learned that I wouldn't get much support there. I felt guilty but for what? Guilt paralyzes the ego. At the same time another part of me knew I hadn't been at fault. Now I know that these conflicts were building a large fund of rage in me.

I narrowed my associations to those playmates I could trust, most of them girls. I always had pets, mostly dogs. They were a great comfort to me. Somewhere around eight or nine I could go by myself to visit down the block to nearby neighbors or even on the other side of town. I went to Sunday school by myself. This was some difference from today's safety concerns! I could go alone down to Ben Small's cafe and candy store. Of the three possibilities in our town, he had the best penny candy. Almost always, Ben would be sitting on one of the counter stools, chewing tobacco and shifting a handful of silver coins from one hand to the other. In the winter, he would turn his head half way around and spit across the room onto the hot side of a pot-bellied stove. It caused a great hiss, much to my delight. With the middle-part in his hair, I was reminded of Ben years later, when I saw a photograph of H.L. Mencken.

I liked to have Ben's wife Ola or Oly wait on me because she put a little extra candy into the small white paper bag. I liked many of the older people in town. They were kind to me and seemed to like me. I had special friends among my father's patients. His office was at one end of our house. He had a large practice and patients might have to wait an hour or two to see him. They would share their lunches with me, such goodies as home cured boiled ham, fried chicken, home made pie and cake and fruits from their trees.

I remember very well a day—the first one after school was over for the summer. My mother said I could go by myself to visit the Pages. Mrs. Page had worked for my mother as long as I could remember. Not regularly, but she did particular jobs like the weekly cleaning, paperhanging, and baking angel food cakes for Mother to take to the Eastern Star suppers. The Pages, Ezra and Ella, were just about the best people I have ever known. They didn't have much themselves, but whatever they had if you needed it, it was yours. Ezra worked a small farm belonging to his neighbors the Fishers. Often in the summer just awakening I would hear Ezra whistling on his way to do the milking and the morning chores. To me it was a reassuring sign that the day was beginning right. He grew corn, some wheat and hay for the horses and other livestock. They kept four or five milk cows and one or two horses. This was before there were many tractors, and besides the farm wasn't big enough for that. They sold their share of the milk to people in the town and the rest to the creamery. I stayed with them when my folks went out of town or to some late meeting. This particular summer Ezra had jokingly asked me if I want to help him thin corn. This was his good good-natured way of making conversation or getting a rise out of me. I think he was surprised when I quickly accepted.

On almost the first day of summer vacation I was off to find him and begin work. It was the first serious sustained all day effort I had ever made. We both worked steadily, wasting no time quickly walking down each row, and hill-by-hill pulling out all the young corn plants but one or two. Lunch was peanut butter sandwiches and milk under the shade of a tree beside the field. We worked about nine or ten hours and finished a ten acre field. I was tired but very happy. I had done something well. Ezra was both pleased and surprised. The whole day had gone peacefully and pleasantly. I did a few other chores with him that summer and the next. This and their kindness affirmed me in a way that nothing up to then had done. They always made me feel that I was the greatest kid ever. Long after when I had difficulties with people at work who were neither kind nor decent I would remember the Pages and be glad that I had known them, decent and good people. I had a new confidence from that work and the success of it. I hadn't by any means put it all together yet, but it was the beginning of seeing a way of escape from home. However the escape and emancipation process took a long time and several false starts.

I was growing up, at least physically and, less rapidly, mentally. I had my first menstrual period just as I turned twelve. I knew what was happening to me but only barely in spite of all the medical books I had read. Like many other things at that time of her life, I remember standing and listening to my mother telling Mrs. Page about it and bemoaning the fact that it had come so soon. "Oh, I was hoping it wouldn't happen so soon!" Something inside me shriveled and tried to hide. What had I done wrong?

I entered High School that fall in Fayette, Ohio, a town five miles from us—new school, new activities, new people, to make or not to make friends and to prepare for college. My mother was ill or half ill. She had an infected jaw from an incompetent tooth extraction. It remained undiscovered for some time and was difficult to treat because for one thing there were no antibiotics then. She was miserable, but there was no one else to drive me to and from school. I felt it as a terrible imposition, and I only half wanted to go anyway. I finished the first two years without distinction. I completed the assignments. I liked the literature courses and did the math and science stuff because I had to. I was being prepared to be a physician. I had never heard of any other possibility for me and I had not been taught to think independently or have any opinions about my education. I never heard of any other possibility mentioned. In the second grade I had written some poems, which the teacher praised highly, telling my mother that this was poetry. It had never occurred to me that I could choose my own vocation. By the time I was six someone asked me what I was going to be when I grew up. I parrot-like stated that I was going to be a doctor. I had a second cousin, a year older than I, who was in my high school class. His folks expected him to go into music. His mother had been a music teacher. He was good at math and the best piano player around. He did go to Oberlin College and graduated in music. Soon after he came home after graduation he suffered a severe depression and ended being a bookkeeper. Years later at my mother's funeral I could hardly believe what I saw. Here was a middle-aged man wrapped in sadness, a solemn stranger, who only half greeted me. Hardly anything was left of the cheerful youth I had known. Sometimes it is more painful to perceive the suffering of others than to experience one's own. We have no control over it and no way of dealing directly with it. Our observations almost immediately go into imagination and distort the reality. Only his facial features told me this was the same boy I had known in his youth.

Mother finally gave up driving me to high school. In my junior year she found a place for me to stay in Fayette. These people, a Mother and daughter were too much like some of the people in my hometown, ignorant and dull. I gained twenty pounds on the starch and meat diet, and learned to roll and smoke coffee cigarettes. Of course my grades suffered. Mother found another place for me to stay with an Eastern Star sister who put me on salads. When her other boarder, a young man in his thirties, made a pass at me, she gracefully, but firmly put him in his place. It was the kind of affirmation that I needed.

I had gone off to high school, not knowing some things I should have. I simply wasn't told anything by either of my parents about sex. I had no real picture of the male sexual anatomy. Daddy's copy of Gray's Anatomy hadn't been much help. I had never been to a museum nor seen any Greek sculpture, which would certainly have enlightened me. I suppose if I had had much curiosity about it I would have found out. I remember the older brother of a summertime playmate had discovered he could terrify us by taking off his pants and chase us round and round the house, and if he caught us, peeing on us. But we were so frightened that neither his brother nor I ever looked at his lower parts. I had seen our dog have puppies, but I never asked how it happened. The sophomore biology class never mentioned anything above frogs and fish. My mother had me so frightened about men that I thought they were a special species out to do women in. I had never asked how they were going to do this.

The class parties and dating if you can call it that, started in my senior year. Dating consisted of two or more couples riding around in one of the classmate's father's automobile all afternoon, or going to a movie. I began to spend a few weekends with the daughter of one of my parents' friends in a nearby but larger town. I dated some of her high school friends who were much more sophisticated than my high school crowd. I was so starved for affection and so ignorant of what a sexual pass was, that I came very close to the real thing several times. When this friend saw what a pushover I was she gave me a serious no-nonsense talk about what would happen to me. It wasn't that I didn't have sexual feelings; I had had them for a long time. I just never connected the whole thing together.

In my senior year I had my first real crush, on a boy in my class. One night in late fall he took me up to his folks' cabin on the lake, but he was so inexperienced and so frightened that nothing happened except a few kisses. Puppy love it was called. I had a few dates with the brother of a high school chum. We did harmless things like going to the movies in Toledo or to the amusement park at the Toledo zoo. One night after a wonderful day there we arrived home at midnight my mother had gone out looking for me. My Uncle Herbert, who was living with us, was standing in the driveway as we pulled into the drive. My mother and father were so afraid that something would happen to me, which would bring shame on them that they did almost unforgivable things to me. After one of these dates, they would get me in the 'den' a small room off the living room and question me. Where, exactly, had we been? What did we do? Did he do anything to me? Who was with us? Where, exactly, did we go? My mother finally became so anxious about my activities that she persuaded my father to examine me to see if I was still a virgin. What she would have done had I not been, I don't know. I can only say that only a loving and patient husband can cure the effects of an experience like this.

While I had learned to some extent how to think I didn't do much of it for long time. During those last miserable years at home when conditions were so bad and I saw no solutions in sight I must told myself not to think about it. In my high school years I lived almost entirely in the present. I grasped at every opportunity to have a good time. Only when I was forced to consider the future did I actively think about it. My grades went down in my junior year. The teachers reminded me that I would not be accepted in any accredited school unless they improved. I studied a little harder but without enthusiasm. I was programmed to prepare for college, to go, to study, to become a physician. I tried to do that. The message was that one did everything expecting it to be difficult, joyless, and because it was one's duty. There was another side to me however. The unrewarded, unaffirmed child had not been assuaged. I wanted to be liked, accepted, and I wanted diversion. I wanted to play, to be sociable, to make real friends.

College

At sixteen I managed to escape, much to my mother's credit as I now see it. She pushed me out of the nest, and out of that miserable little town as soon as she could. She started me in school at five, and she insisted that I skip grades when I could. I graduated from high school at sixteen in a class of twenty-one. I enrolled the University of Michigan with its 15,000 students. It would have been difficult to find a more unprepared individual. To register for freshman English was an ordeal. One could complete a good deal of rearranging one's schedule and find the section had closed. There were no guidance or counseling services. I couldn't adjust to living in a dormitory with 399 women. There were too many distractions. I had not considered what I would like to study or that I could be allowed to. The only course I liked was the second semester English, a writing course taught by Professor Abbot who also managed the university radio station. He liked the pieces I wrote and encouraged me. Yet nothing broke through the mold that said I would become a physician. I had never asked myself "What do you want?" Ann Arbor was an overwhelming experience. I had less than a C-average. I knew I did not want to return for another year.

In retrospect I believe that I was slowly and painfully admitting to myself and to my parents that I didn't want to be a doctor. The further truth was that my sense of myself had been so mangled that when it came to making an adult and important decision I couldn't do it. I knew I was miserable. While fearful of losing whatever respect and regard they had for me my overwhelming negative response to the university convinced them. I was sure I had disgraced my parents. What would people say either to them or behind their backs about my failure? The sense of failure remained with me for months. I couldn't plan for my future. My sister, much older and having successfully navigated the university experience came up with a plan. I would come to live with her in Cleveland and attend Flora Stone Mather College of Western Reserve University. I must have thought that because the college was smaller I could become interested in science and the faculty would be helpful. It soon became apparent that my conclusions were not correct. Trigonometry and chemistry did not interest me, but I pursued the program with a kind of frantic determination. In this new situation I looked everywhere for approval, friendship and kindly attitudes. At the same time I was hypersensitive to the least show of disfavor or rejection and made a quick withdrawal if it appeared. I was not able to defend my opinions or beliefs.

I didn't get off to a favorable start in my initial interview with the Dean of the college. She was the archetype of all deans I have heard or read of. She was plain to the point of homeliness, stiff and severe in her posture and expression. At the required interview I appeared with a chip out of a front tooth. It showed when I smiled and I smiled a lot then, mostly out of nervousness. She asked me how I had received it. I explained that I had attended the county fair as almost everyone did since it was one of the big events of the year. As I was getting into one of the amusement park rides the operator brought the bar down before I was seated. It hit my mouth and chipped a piece from my tooth. She looked at me unsmiling, and that I took it to be disapproval. It was as if to say 'a likely story,' or 'what were you doing in such a place?' or God alone knows what she thought. The signals were not reassuring for a green country girl in whose mind the dean of a college must be an important someone. If she didn't like me it was going to be even tougher to succeed here. This interview killed whatever enthusiasm I had for this institution. During the semester I made friends with two social workers who boarded where I did. One day I happened to meet them in the halls of the University medical school. Knowing I was in a premed program they offered to show me the autopsy room. We were just outside the door into it. They said "Come on we'll show you around in there". An unbelievable fear bordering on terror grabbed me. I was afraid of all those dead bodies. Suppose they weren't dead and would rise up and start talking to me? The question of being a physician or not being a physician was settled right then and there. I had to get out of there and out of the college. I left as soon as I could at the end of the semester.

During this time at the college I began to draw. I have forgotten what started me doing this. Perhaps I'd seen some drawings or paintings at the Cleveland Museum or a private show of someone's work. The college was only a few blocks from the Museum and the Cleveland School of Art. My first visit to the Museum with my sister was a delight. It was my introduction to art and the beginning of a lifelong interest. I went there whenever I could get a little time. There was no admission charge then, and no crowds on weekdays, even for the major exhibitions.

I now had behind me two unsuccessful attempts to fulfill my parents' ambitions for me. It was at last becoming clear to me that I didn't want to study medicine. On the strength of my drawing my sister, not knowing what to do, suggested perhaps I should enroll in the Art School. This was a wonderful escape at last—well not quite yet. The first two years I applied myself enthusiastically, learning the basic techniques, drawing, perspective, watercolor painting, working in clay. There wasn't another student there who had had as little art training as I. They had all taken courses in high school while I was working away at science. It was all right because this was a very laid back place in one sense but with a very adult approach in another. You could work hard and achieve, or just get by with the assignments. In either case they would take your money. No one berated you or urged you. The world of art opened for me and for many years enriched my life in a way that nothing else had.

I began to become acquainted with the other students. One of them was a young woman of exceptional talent. She had been drawing and painting most of her life. She helped me to see and to understand what it was we were studying. She had a scholarship from the school. She also played the piano with great delicacy and feeling. Her family was in its own way as strange as mine. She was an only child. There were, besides her mother and father, an Aunt, her mother's sister, who lived with them. They lived in a plain but good old house, which her parents owned. They were respectable, threadbare, working people. These were the years of the great depression. Her father had been out of a job for several of them. The Aunt cheerfully supported them with a job she went to six days a week. My friend had long dark ash-blond hair, which she wore in a style similar to Elizabeth Barrette Browning. It made her look far older than her eighteen years. I persuaded her to cut it and actually I cut it for her. She was pleased and so was everyone else in the family. It was such a mild and gentle family that I suspect if they hadn't liked it they would only have murmured to themselves. My family would have blurted out their dislike at once. I suspect it was this gentleness that attracted me to her. She was the closest friend I had had up to then.

For the first two years of school we spent time together when we could. But when I returned to school to begin my third year I turned away from her. I avoided her. I didn't know then exactly why. I couldn't follow and identify my feelings then. I began to associate with an entirely different group of girls, social types for whom school was a passage between prep school and marriage. I understand now that my unconscious was sending up a clear warning to me. I was very fond of her and I was so needy for love and she certainly valued our friendship and our relationship so much that it could have become something neither of us would have ultimately been happy or satisfied with. Convention had been too deeply implanted in both of us. It hurt her at the time, and I could not explain it because I did not understand it myself.

In third and fourth year my friends were more socially inclined. Among my new friends was one I liked and had spent several weekends with at her home. She was the opposite of me in disposition and physical type—small, blond, vivacious and quick-tempered. Her father was an executive in one of the rubber companies in Akron. She was fun—something I still had not had enough of. She knew people I would never have met. She had one friend, an older man from New York, who was, I think, a theatrical agent. When she was going to spend an evening with him, she took me along. Why, I am not sure. He was a harmless sort, who, it seemed to me liked the company of young women. He took us to the best restaurants for dinner, after which we would go nightclubbing until two or three in the morning. Usually we ended up at the Turf Club to listen to Rose Murphy play the piano. He would buy each of us a large spray of gardenias. We all got pretty high, and waking next morning and smelling those flowers turned me off gardenias for life. These were harmless evenings except that some of the clubs we frequented sometimes featured acts just on the borderline of decency. I could never bring myself to look at them. Then toward the end of our last year my blond friend met the man of her dreams. Her father had come *out* of the labor force and pulled himself up the corporate ladder to a very responsible position. The family hadn't grown socially. Except for good cars, a nice home, and fine clothes, they were still back in the lunch pail part of their life. Her father was one of those rough and tough Irishmen who still stopped off at the local saloon after work. Arriving home after several drinks, he would stagger up the back stairs, a string of expletives issuing from him as he made his way up into the kitchen. It was the same performance every day. It was his idea of a warm and cordial greeting. My friend was like her father, but she had been away at school and had acquired a veneer of refinement, which her sister and brother at home did not have. She was preparing to be an art teacher. When she wasn't working or attending school she was usually sipping on a drink, but I saw her drunk only once,.

She had been seeing a man she had fallen in love with twice and sometimes three times a week. She thought the affair was as serious for him as it was for her.

At about the time we graduated, he announced his engagement to a socially prominent and rich young woman whom none of us knew. I was going out at the time with this man's closest friend, and he didn't know about this woman either.

Of course my friend was devastated, but not enough to stop her from asking me to spend an afternoon with her in Akron. I had no more than entered the living room than she fired off at me exactly in the style of her father. Why hadn't I told her? What kind of friend was I? No one before or since, and that is now fifty-two years, has ever berated me in such a fashion. When I finally comprehended what was happening, I got up and walked out of the house and waited at the end of the drive where someone was to pick me up. She said nothing and did not follow me. About a year later I heard that she had left the family dinner table one Sunday afternoon, gone into her father's room, taken his pistol from a drawer, and blown her head off.

My First Marriage

While the Ann Arbor and Flora Stone Mather experiences had been painful they had shaken me out of my habitual semi-depressed 'hoped for love' condition. What had taken its place was an active, but unhappy half-paralyzed state. I didn't know what I wanted to do or become—actually I didn't want to do anything. Entering art school had been for me like giving a child with nothing to do a piece of paper and a bunch of crayons to fill her time. I was miserably unhappy without even realizing that, probably because I had become used to living in a non-fulfilling environment. It was an impossible position from which to choose a life vocation. It says something about the durability of my disposition that in this state, delicate and easily defeated, I somehow carried on. But even though such a one may survive many adjustments to unfulfilling conditions, eventually cracks begin to appear.

It was my last year in art school. It had been a wonderful respite and a temporary solution while I was trying to discover and locate any talents or inclinations that would lead to a life work. Not that I was ever inclined to talk about my troubles—there was no one in this art milieu who knew much more than I did. Freud and Jung had not made it to the masses in the early thirties. We talked about what we liked or what some of us intended to do, for some making a living and for others filling time before marriage. Our motives for why we were there never came up in our talks. The only goal I was aware of was to avoid going home. In this depression era there were no jobs that I could fill. I wasn't qualified to do anything that was employable. I enjoyed the art training but in accomplishment I was near the bottom of the class.

Then I met a divorced man and his friends, who had similar life styles. Most of them were sales executives or advertising types, either confirmed bachelors or divorced. This man was almost ten years older than I with one failed marriage, now single, and he seemed to like me. I wasn't particularly attracted to him, but marriage was a way to avoid returning home. After we had been married a few weeks I discovered his drinking problem and the bitter consequences of it. He

42

began to stop at a restaurant-bar a few blocks from where we were living for a couple of drinks on his way home from work. It wasn't very long before it was more than a couple of drinks. Drunk he became abusive, and finally one night, heavily intoxicated, he grabbed me around the neck and choked me so severely that with all my strength I could not free myself. Something told me to relax as if unconscious and pray. Almost immediately he relaxed his hands and sat down on his bed. For probably eight hours he sat there alternately muttering incoherently and finally slobbering and vomiting. When he recovered he had no memory of this. A little over a week later he lost his job. There was no place to go except to my home. I thought he could be reformed. Maybe my father could give him something. How little I knew about alcoholism. This was the age of Prohibition. I had heard of whisky when I was younger but I had never seen a drunk. Thinking my parents would be a buffer against his drinking I convinced him to go home with me. Not long after were there I saw it was useless to hope for reform. I said nothing to my father about wanting a divorce. He was in ill health, and after a few weeks he died. After the funeral I convinced my husband to take his clothes and automobile and return to Cleveland to look for a job. I told him I would join him when he found one. The day after he left Mother and I went to the county courthouse in Bryan, and I filed a suit for divorce. Her support for me in this period showed me that odd however her approach to life she did care for me and for my welfare. Love hoped for had taken such a pummeling that for quite a long time it went underground. Mere survival became my need.

World War II

Fortunately, in early 1942 the U. S. Government was hiring for the war effort. They were taking everyone they could get as long as they could read and write and walk. Armed with my Civil Service forms I went to the Tank Automotive Center in the Fisher building just a few blocks from my sister's apartment. They hired me for the personnel department at $1200 per annum. With almost no income tax I was rich. It was going to be a large organization, and two-hundred employees from Washington had arrived a few days before I went to work. There were four women in the personnel department but none of them had been able to get the records and time cards correct so that new people could be paid. It was my first assignment. I spent a couple of weeks surrounded by time cards, transfer papers and per diem forms struggling to get the mess in order. On pay day there had been a lineup because paychecks were incorrect or not there. I straightened it out the best I could. On the next payday my boss, a career civil servant, proudly announced to the Major, her boss, in my presence, that there were no mistakes this time. Ah! At last somebody needed me.

There were other problems. I soon discovered how obnoxious this woman, my boss, could be. On any given day two or three of our all-woman staff could be found in the washroom splashing their tear-stained faces to compose themselves after one of her dressings down. Sometimes even the smallest error in typing would bring on her wrath. None of us had any clear idea how to handle this situation, and no one wanted to stay on if it continued. Finally, after about the third evening of complaining to my sister and wailing about my plight, she abruptly asked me if I had any idea what to do about it. "Not the slightest," I said. "Well I do," she replied. "The next time this happens go back in and tell her how devastated you all are by her tactics." "Oh, I could never do that," I said. "You have to do something," she replied. "You need the money." It was true. Sure enough, the next day it happened again, and after a short period in the washroom calming down I decided to follow my sister's advice. I asked to see my boss. I started out calmly enough about her effect on us and began to give her examples. The more I talked the worse I felt until I just broke down and cried. She was appalled. She had no idea that she was causing such reactions not only in me, but in the rest of the staff. Later, when she told the Major about it, he took it calmly. A regular army officer with a bland no-nonsense exterior, who has come up through the ranks has surely heard and seen about everything connected with the human condition.

There were four or five of us in the personnel department plus my boss and her secretary. That secretary, Betty, was the jewel of the staff. She was just eighteen, a spunky French girl from a large family right there in Detroit. Good-natured and remarkably patient for her age, her dark eyes sparkled when she was amused. This was her first job, and she strove to do it right. Viola, our boss, had her keep the files under the Dewey Decimal System, which I am sure has now been long abandoned. It was one of the most complicated and most detailed system for classifying information I had or have yet seen. It was the official system for the entire War Department at the time and may even have been used by the whole government, for all I ever knew or learned about it. The correspondence, regulations, and administrative rules were minutely classified under headings, sub-headings, sub-sub-headings, *ad infinitum*. I'm sure you could have classified the hairs on a fly's back under the system. About any time you happened to go into her office you could see Betty standing at an open file drawer muttering to herself while pondering the Dewey manual to find a classification for the letter she held in her other hand.

Not long after I arrived in the department, two or three weeks at the most, Viola called me into her office and announced to me that she was being transferred to Washington to be trained as a position analyst. I expressed regret at her going and wished her success. I asked her who would take her place, and in her usual abrupt manner, as if I ought to have known, she replied: "Why you are, of course." I thought she was just being funny, but she assured me that she was serious. I immediately wondered how the rest of the staff would take this, since I was junior to all of them. I needn't have wondered. They didn't like it. I appealed to their patriotism and tried to reassure them that I didn't know beans about supervising people and that I was hypersensitive about telling other people what to do because of my early experience with the hometown kids. They griped from time to time and made sarcastic remarks, but this was not new to me. I saw that it wasn't an organized resistance—just a little bellyaching here and there.

My salary jumped four classifications in six months. About this time the income tax started to increase. Nevertheless I still had more money than I had ever had. We worked long hours, with no overtime pay, and in rather makeshift conditions. But so did everyone else. Then they began to move other personnel out from Washington. The Fisher building was not large enough and we moved downtown to the Union Guardian building. This had been a bank in peacetime, but had been entirely emptied out so that the Tank-Automotive Center's five divisions could be located more or less together. They were making the tanks and testing them at the General Motors proving ground. As the organization became larger, each division had its own administrative officer who reported to a central personnel department on the main floor. I was running into more and more of the military mind. I hadn't a clue as to how it operated. Just to get a first endorsement to a memo worded correctly for some officers so that it could be approved, signed and sent off could take the better part of half a day. Endorsements often consisted of fewer than ten lines, but with some of the officers you had to go over it word by word. It was wearing and, I thought, ridiculous. We had many officers who were not regular army. They were called up from the reserve when the war effort began. I realize they were as uncertain as we were about some forms and procedures and therefore over cautious. I'm sure no such nonsense existed on the battlefields.

It was a life of long hours of work and little play or time for it. I went for several years without a date but so did a lot of the other women in our office. If there were attractive officers who were available, I missed them. Besides, I was more gun-shy than every after my unfortunate marriage. I was aware of the situation and the dullness of my life. On my twenty-ninth birthday, sitting at the breakfast table, it all came over me at once. My youth was passing and I hadn't had very much fun. I didn't see much prospect of it either. About 1944 my sister again moved to take a job in Flint, Michigan, leaving me with a two-bedroom apartment. I needed to find some roommates to help with expenses. Two women who had recently come to Detroit from Washington heard about my apartment. We made a deal and they both moved in.

They had boyfriends who were officers, reserve, married and far from home. My boarders used to stay out pretty late. I never paid much attention to their comings and goings. The men kept trying to fix me up with some of their friends. We had a sort of custom established that we would invite people in for Sunday dinner. The officer boyfriends were regulars. From time to time they would bring along some fellow officer they thought I might like. I remember one in particular who certainly tried in about the grossest way I have ever been approached to get me to pay attention to him and accept him. Just before dinner, often when the food was already on the table, he would decide to chase me around the table and "get at me" as he would call it. I was really terrified of him, as he was so big and so uncouth. He was not totally unintelligent even though he appeared to be. He was a graduate engineer from Texas A & M, but he hadn't the slightest idea how to approach a woman (or perhaps this is the Texas model). It might be a little exaggerated, but he was a pretty fair example of the male talent that was available there and then. There was another type of the exact opposite—repressed, sexually fearful, fat, and tongue-tied.

Here I was, approaching thirty, and I still had not met any really eligible men. Part of this, of course, had to be blamed on the war. I also felt sure I wasn't moving in the right circles. Later on, when I moved to Washington at the end of the war, it was pretty much the same. While still in Detroit I got so bored with the government's way of doing things and the people, that when offered a job in private industry, I took it. It wasn't any better, but I held on, hoping that something better would come along.

I had made some female friends, most of whom were in administrative positions in the various divisions of the Center, as I was. We would have dinner together when we could or take a weekend cruise on the lakes, or go swimming on a Sunday at one of the small lakes outside Detroit. One or two of them had pretty nice boyfriends, temporary, of course, for the duration only. These friendships helped me in several ways. These women were stylish, attractive, had good social lives before the war. We exchanged experiences about our lives, including the amusing and funny things that had happened to us. We had nicknames for each other. One was known as "Madame Administrator," the best job in the group, another was "Miss Priss," because she was anything but, and so on. I was called "The Brain." Our jobs were widely enough distributed so that we pretty much covered the whole organization, and we knew when a new face appeared among the men. It didn't help. They just weren't in our installation.

One of the friends I had made early in my empl0yment there had gone to the War Labor Board's Detroit office as their Administrative Officer. When she heard that I had gone out into industry she called me and offered me a job in her organization. She couldn't have done that if I had still been with the War Depart-

ment because it was against the wartime regulations for anyone in the government war effort to snatch anyone from another defense agency. I accepted
quickly. The private company I was with published technical manuals. My job
was to keep the artists producing the illustrations on time. It was hopeless from
the beginning. Artists have their own particular prejudices and they are not easy
to dislodge. I failed miserably because I was not aggressive enough. My successor,
a product of the Ford Motor Company was a 'I don't care if you like it or not the
work has to get our fast' person. That attitude got out the manuals.

The War Labor Board's Detroit office had a small staff and was practically free
of politics. The professionals were educated individuals, mostly economists, labor
specialists, and lawyers. It was a much looser organization than I had been in, but
it did some very effective work. I went there in late 1944 or early 1945. Everyone
expected that the board's business would soon wind down. I began to prepare a
reduction in force program to help reduce staff and if possible find suitable jobs
for those who had to go. It was much more successful than we expected. On the
basis of this, I was asked to come to Washington to the headquarters personnel
office and help set up their reduction in force program. It was even better than
the Detroit office as far as the people, who were educated, enjoyable, warm
human beings. Washington was such uplift after Detroit that I couldn't believe
it. I was to be in Washington temporarily, but I stayed on and worked there for
ten more years.

At first I stayed in a small hotel for several weeks with the woman who had
hired me. Then I lived in the Virginia home of the Assistant Director of Personnel. We used to eat breakfast every morning listening to Arthur Godfrey. It was a
great beginning for the day. I suppose he knew from many sources what an uplift
and joy he was at that hour in those circumstances, for all of us war-weary souls. I
finished my work with the Board and was trying to place myself in a job. I had
applied at the Marriott Hotel Shops for a personnel job. They turned me down. I
have always thought it was because I had earlier belonged to a union. I had
resigned my membership when it became an issue whether the union supported
the withdrawal of American troops from Germany, as I recall, leaving the Russians there. The union was for withdrawal, but I was not. I thought the Russians
should withdraw and the Americans stay. After all we had been the decisive factor
in the victory. Something was rotten in Denmark. I resigned. I wasn't going to
belong to an organization that had such a lopsided policy. I guess the Marriotts
had not heard the second part of my union history. I'm very grateful now that it

was as it was, because fortuitous events were about to happen which determined the outcome and course of the rest of my life.

I had applied to the Central Intelligence Agency, the then Central Intelligence Group. It was one of the few organizations that was hiring anyone. I had no idea that the clearance would take so long. They wanted me in the agency for an administrative officer position in one of the divisions. I waited and waited. In spite of the fact that my whole life had been spent in a small geographical area of the USA with no foreign trips, friends, or connections, it took forever to clear me. My severance pay from the Board had ended, I was part owner of a George-town house, which I had bought with a friend from Detroit days, and I had no savings to help me. It was a time of real material insecurity. Something I had never really experienced. I had always known where and when money to live on would come from. Now I was beginning to wonder how I was going to eat.

I shall be forever grateful to the YMCA for the part-time job they found for me at their building on K Street. The staff there, all of them, lived what they believed, and were probably the best example I will ever see of the Christian ethic in action. They understood my plight very well and helped me all they could. It was a kind of fun job and had its amusing aspects. As evening supervisor of the building, I was to keep the sailors from taking their girls up into the loft at the top of the building. I was also to monitor the evening news program in the main lounge. The Y had installed a large radio there and every evening at news time the elderly ladies who frequented the Y would gather there with a few old men sprinkled among them. I soon discovered they could be classified into two distinct groups: those who wanted to listen to Huntley and Brinkley and those who wanted to listen to Fulton Lewis, Jr. Each faction was strongly opinionated in favor of its program. This was probably the principal reason I was hired was to keep peace in the lounge during the news broadcasts. At the beginning I found members of the two groups actually going up to the radio and turning the others' program off and theirs on. A noisy squabble would ensue. We worked out a system whereby each could hear his program on alternate nights. An uneasy and watchful silence prevailed. Peace was restored.

At last my security clearance came through, and I reported to the personnel office in one of the temporary buildings near the Potomac River not far from the Watergate Inn. It was a lovely setting. It backed onto an inner gem of a garden court, surrounded by other more or less permanent buildings, which I suppose are now gone. In the spring numerous trees and other plants in the court would produce a beautiful array of colorful blooms. On the other side and along the water one could stroll or sit on the lush grass in the warm sunshine during lunch hour. The Watergate Inn was a great place to lunch on special occasions. It was an interval, a pause, a time for recovering from the war. While plans were being made, and new enterprises had begun, the great surge of expansion and activity that is Washington today had only just started. The details of my first days and months there are vague. I had been hired for a division that had not yet been formed, but professionals to staff it were being cleared and reporting every week. If there was an organization chart for it, I had never seen it. I just did what I was told to do each day and hoped that things would soon be clearer and have some shape. It was eventually established. I began to function as I had been hired to do. The first head of this division was a Lt. Col. Whitely. He wasn't there very long. It was very difficult to find qualified individuals who were willing to work under such tight security restrictions. Often they weren't qualified because the combination of intelligence officer and knowledge of subject to be covered had never existed in this country. The British had much more of a history of this kind of work, but I suspect they had their problems too. It took a rare bird, a kind of generalist who had some knowledge of many different areas of human activity and a specific and thorough knowledge of a specialty. Ideally people who had worked in the Office of Strategic Services in World War II who could see the relation of the one to the other.

I have no idea how many employees were in the agency at that time. Compared to later it was barely a nucleus. In the beginning I found it to be interesting and stimulating. This was a new venture for America, and precedents for many things that needed to be done did not exist. Fortunately there were already in the agency a number of able people who had been with the Office of Strategic Services and were also of recognized competence internationally. We were still relatively free of the restraints of a set of rules and regulations characteristic of well-organized bureaucracies. The agency was not under the restrictions of civil service in hiring their employees. Headquarters would hire a man to head our division. He would come on duty with a lot of enthusiasm and ideas, and a good knowledge of the subject he was hired to deal with. After a time, varying from several months to two years, he would leave. I don't think anyone lasted much longer than that. He would find the security restrictions too much or he couldn't deal with some of the crazy geniuses, who thought up ways to carry out his ideas in the field. There were times in between when we had no director. Morale would be low, and having the longest tenure of anyone there I would try to cheer up what staff we had. Only once did anyone, realizing our condition, come down from the front office to cheer us up. General Wright was the Assistant to the Director, and he appeared one day looking for someone on the staff to talk to. He was referred to me. He tried to reassure me, and I was to convey his reassurance to the others, explaining that they were doing everything possible to find a new director. It was a good and thoughtful gesture, and we all appreciated it.

CIA in the Post-War World

Directors continued to come and go during my almost ten years there. I got along fairly well with most of them. Some I liked very much and learned a lot from them just because their approach to life was often so different from mine. Sometimes because of the nature of their work ludicrous situations arose over which we doubled up in laughter. I remember a comment by the secretary of one of the directors just after an applicant for a job interview had left the office. She said "I would not be surprised to see a crocodile come in here some morning while I'm sitting here typing."

It was customary for any paper what was written on a particular problem or status of a situation to be reviewed in conference with the Director and a senior analyst competent in the subject of the paper. We had a man who, while he was technically competent in his field, had no intelligence analysis experience. He was strictly a sedentary indoor type, very pale skin and puffy fat. He was slow speaking, very mild and gentle. His turn came for a session with his senior analyst and the Director. This took place in the Director's office with the writer of the paper sitting between the Director and the senior analyst. These could be very tough sessions because what was proposed was an initial plan or means of obtaining vital intelligence information from the field. Every detail had to be looked at and the conclusions questioned minutely. On this occasion they left the door open during the whole proceeding. In the course of the morning I had several occasions during the course of my work to pass by the door. I couldn't hear them but at one point I saw the hapless writer of the paper pause and wipe his brow. I told the Director later the scene reminded me of a marshmallow between two forks being roasted at a picnic.

I gave a wholly negative vote to only one of the Directors. We had just had a very able man who preceded him, but he had left because he couldn't stand the security restrictions and the bureaucracy. On his first day on the job this tactless and stupid individual in a staff meeting of all the professionals without warning me and in my presence announced that I would no longer be Administrative

Officer. He said he did not want any women on his staff in positions of such responsibility. Of course this was a terrible shock to me, who had always had excellent efficiency ratings and had actually been a pillar of strength through the many changes that the division had undergone. I was sure he had the support of the personnel division or he could not have carried his plan through. Today it would be impossible for such a thing to happen. I applaud the women's organizations for their efforts to eliminate such prejudicial practices, though like everything else the change has been abused.

There was a big question where to assign me. I was now one of the longest tenured employees in the agency, and I did not want to go to the covert operations side. I was finally put out to the National Security Agency, a sister organization responsible for communications intelligence, of which I knew nothing. I was the only one of several CIA people there who had no experience in this field. So I was to supervise the rest of the CIA staff and take care of their administrative needs. It was a made-up job to have some place to put me out of the way. The regular communications people resented us. We were paid more than they were, and they had to fit us into their already crowded space. They were considerably less than cooperative in helping us learn. It was a miserable situation, especially for me, since I had considered making intelligence my career. I was out there in the country in Virginia about a year when someone pulled some strings for me. To this day I am not quite sure which one of two or three of my associates or former associates in the agency did this. I was reclaimed and brought back into Washington to do a study of the Soviet Academy of Science of which we knew relatively little. I had already been sent to the Georgetown School of Languages to learn Russian, at which I did rather poorly. Putting together pieces of information from both unclassified and classified sources was interesting in its way, but far from absorbing. The truth was that the shock of having been pushed out of a responsible and interesting job, only because of my gender, had burned out my energy and enthusiasm for any work in that place. The continuing stress from the unstable condition of the division due to the many changing directors had had its negative effect. But as with so many events in my life, it was only much later that I recognized what it had done to me. I supervised six or seven people working with me on this project. I gave a couple of briefings to agency personnel. I worked on parts of the study, but I was marking time for what I didn't know. I didn't look beyond the next day, as far as my daily bread was involved.

But there was a big difference in me now from before my transfer. I tried to analyze the problem, and I asked myself what was wrong besides this man's attitude toward women. I knew I had some faults. I was impatient with the stupidity and lack of thought in others. I was somewhat aggressive, but this was magnified in the eyes of the weak men with whom I sometimes had to deal. They found me difficult and there were enough of them to reinforce each other's opinions. I had had enough of these troubles that I seriously wanted to understand them so I could do something about it. In a moment of enlightenment I said to myself "but you are the common denominator of all of them." What soon followed was the realization that I needed help from outside. I could not help myself. Help, I found, was at hand and in two rather different forms.

I had made friends with a young woman in the agency who was an analyst in another division. We often had lunch together and discussed our problems, mostly problems with people. Hers were a little different from mine, but not that much. I told her of my momentous insight and the realization that followed. She in turn told me about a study, a philosophy, she had recently become interested in through a wartime friend who had been in the OSS with her. Her friend's husband was leader of a group studying the works of G.I. Gurdjieff and P.D. Ouspensky, which was purported to be a means of self-realization. She had already received some benefit from it, she told me. I was interested and anxious to meet this man because I wanted to begin to find out the meaning of my life. At about the same time I had to move into another apartment, which I shared with another woman whom I didn't know too well. As I later learned she had had a severe depression, which she had successfully overcome with the help of a psychiatrist in her hometown, Baltimore. I didn't care for this woman's life style, and I moved as soon as I could, but I did go to her psychiatrist, Dr. Jacob H. Conn. I know only a few of the countless people he helped, but he helped those I know so successfully that they could resume their lives as normal functioning human beings. He was the ideal choice at that moment for my battered ego to provide support for my "Love Hoped For."

Some interesting and good people in our division were not happy with all the changes they had lived through along with me. One of the Directors had the idea that we should have a wide spectrum of talents, which included the social or cultural sciences. This brought in recent PhD's in several disciplines, and these people brought an attitude toward problems, which tended to diffuse tension as they viewed situations with tolerance and humor. Their time in the agency was for them a passing experience. They were young and would go on to other opportunities in business and academe. A few didn't know what their ultimate goal would be. I had become acquainted with one of these soon after his group was transferred to our division from the War Department. He was among about five civilians and two or three officers who appeared one day and needed space. Later on when they were settled in there was a big move from the central personnel office to be sure the divisions had central files or at least had begun to consolidate the files of the groups into one central place. This newly transferred group was specializing in Soviet nuclear intelligence. Because they not only had sensitive intelligence information but also "Restricted" atomic energy information, they had operated more or less independently prior to coming with us. They had retained a good deal of that attitude after joining us. It was understood that the atomic energy Restricted Data was to be kept strictly away from other personnel in the agency. Although I wasn't cleared for atomic energy information it fell to me to try to obtain for consolidation what files they might have, if, indeed, they had any. No one was sure, but I was sent down to try to find out. It was a little like sending a mouse to petition a bunch of hungry cats. They didn't scratch me, but I was met with a deviously clever silence. I was referred to a young man named Charles, their brightest analyst, whom I had met only briefly before. I remember nothing now of our conversation, but at the end of an hour I went away empty handed. Even worse, I was half way down the hall to my office before I realized it! I don't remember any other such defeat in all my working life. I had to report my failure to my boss, the Director, who doubled up with laughter. The personnel department didn't find it amusing. The issue of centralized files was not pursued very seriously after that.

The Gurdjieff Work

Actually what was really wanted was for the new group's information to be available to the rest of the division because they had been incredibly accurate in their intelligence estimates in a highly critical area. It turned out that there were practically no files. They carried the information around in their heads, or what little they had in writing was in this young man's nearly illegible handwriting. Later I shared an office with him and we became good friends. Our friendship blossomed out of his struggle to find dried tarragon leaves for his attempts at making béarnaise sauce for his steaks. Washington was still suffering from post-war scarcities, but I was able to find a bottle, which I placed on his desk one morning before he arrived. He was impressed by my thoughtfulness and was grateful. After he left the agency I had lunch or dinner with him once in a while. When I became interested in the Gurdjieff work and thought there was something to it, I told him about it. He then read Ouspensky's book *In Search of the Miraculous*, but when he came to have dinner with me I noticed he was uneasy and restive. After dinner he began to talk about the book, which he had brought with him. The part about half way through it where Ouspensky describes the influence of the moon on man upset him. After having dinner with me and telling me this, I didn't see him again for about six months. I didn't call him to ask what happened, as I would not have thought it proper. He would have thought I was running after him and this would have put him off even more. I was right. When he did surface it turned out that he had been studying Hinduism, Buddhism, and Christianity. I guess he wanted to sort out what he did and didn't believe. Growing up in Tulare, California, he had been very active in the Congregational Church, even participating in their Junior Pastor Program. But as with me, he had decided there had to be more to life than what he had found so far or the game wasn't worth the candle. He meant to give it a good try before he gave up. Now he was back, and because of the great change for the better he recognized in me since I had been studying what came to be known as "The Work," he asked to meet the man who was leading the group in Washington.

How casually we arrange an occasion for two people to meet because we think it is important or for some unsubstantiated reason. Its significance is almost unknown to us nor its importance in our lives. It is as if a few tufts of brain cells get together to be loud enough to project the idea. I thought the lunch I arranged for my friend Charles to meet Hugh Ripman, the Gurdjieff group leader was such an event. I introduce this term "Group Leader" here, and you'll hear it a lot later on. That lunch on that spring day at the Watergate Inn turned both Charles and me in another direction. It was the beginning of our life together. It led us to take the first steps on a frustrating and often annoying quest. Of its difficulty neither of us had any idea.

During the lunch I felt like an observer at a tennis match. The conversation consisted of frank and probing questions from Charles and equally sharp and decisive replies from Ripman. Charles wanted to know what he might be getting into, and our Group Leader very much wanted to meet the man in whom I had become so interested. I was so busy turning my head from first one to the other that I could hardly eat my lunch. They went after each other like two evenly matched wrestlers, each trying to find the weak spot in the other to deliver the telling point. It wasn't a long lunch, but it was so intense I felt as if someone had given me a shot of adrenalin. Charles was satisfied by the replies he received and decided to try the Gurdjieff work. He began to attend the meetings.

Some form of physical work was connected with this system. Our leader, Hugh Ripman, had a place outside Vienna, Virginia, where we would come on Sunday to do gardening, housework, cooking, or whatever was seasonal. During this time of working one was to try to observe oneself, to collect impressions of how one was, or how one behaved. This was called self-observation and "remembering one's self". The idea was that if one could do this consistently, one would obtain over a period of time enough information to know ones self. This self-knowledge was calculated to produce a shock sufficient to cause one to change one's behavior. Certain undesirable characteristics would be put aside and one's good or positive features would be strengthened. The physical work was very tiring. It was meant to be, because it was believed in the system that one's resistance to seeing oneself was lowered with physical fatigue. Also that one's manifestation under pressure became louder and more self-evident.

Our Group Leader was an old-time Ouspensky man. He had been through a very hard school in England, where they often worked all night on some of the

Work projects. Consequently he was not easy on us. I was still working at the Agency and putting in nearly a full week on the Gurdjieff Work. I had moved temporarily to live with Mr. Ripman and his family for a period of four months in early 1953 prior to our going to Europe together. It was exhausting, and I could barely keep up at the Agency. We would be up until very late at night. Little sleep was supposed to assist the process of remembering oneself. It had the opposite effect for me. I was so tired I was just barely making sense in daily transactions, and I knew it. However, I wasn't so tired as not to notice things in the family relationships, which upset me. I asked myself how a person could be so supposedly "developed" and be so blind in his relationships. I thought both his wife and their small son suffered because of this. I became very upset, and yet I felt there was no one I could talk to about it. His wife seemed to be unable to make decisions—even the small ones. I took over the meal preparation on the days we worked there. I remained in touch with her for many years after that summer and she remained more or less like this to the end of her life. Neither the Ripmans ever called their son by his given name. They called him "Boy". Their son never called his father by any of the customary names—instead it was a distortion of some kind and came out as "Didley".

In the middle of this, an old friend from Wayne University days came to Washington and called me. She had gone on to become a physician and then a psychoanalyst. We had kept in touch and saw each other perhaps once or twice a year. She was coming to Washington, and I asked her to come out to the farm and have dinner with us. She looked the whole situation over, as I had hoped she would. On the drive back into town after dinner, she let herself out. She was appalled by Ripman's treatment of his son, condescending and lacking feeling. But of course she was most interested in my welfare, and without being asked she informed me that I was depressed and sufficiently depressed that I ought to seek professional help. I realize now that I had been depressed most of my life. I think of it now as a restraining, paralyzing weight that kept me from functioning at anywhere near full power. That power, which I see in psychic terms as fueling self-confidence, was being used to support the depression, certainly a no-self-confidence manifestation. I listened very carefully to what she had to say and decided she was right. She had known me for over fifteen years in a number of situations, and she was professionally qualified, moreover there was nothing in it for her except friendship.

My stay with the Ripman family ended in July, and we all went off to Europe together. I was to spend a week on the French Riviera with them and then go alone to Italy. Our trip started in Paris where I first realized how exquisite and how delicious food could be. Even in the smallest dens of eating-places an omelet could be a trip to heaven. We traveled in a 1949 Pontiac, if I remember correctly, which belonged to the famous Cordon Bleu cook, Dionne Lucas. We were to use it for our trip, and she would pick it up later in Paris. That automobile was a disaster. Our first stop was lunch at Chartres on a Sunday. The restaurant was filled with French families, napkins tucked into their collars, busily working over a large platter of prawns, followed by roast chicken, and ending with wild strawberries and cream. We ordered the same and attacked it with as much enthusiasm as the rest of the clientele. Even today, fifty plus years later, when I think of that roast chicken I enjoy it all over again.

After lunch we walked around the town and into the cathedral. Booklet in hand, we worked our way around the interior, looking carefully at the details of the structure and the ornament imposed on it. I was impressed by the majesty of its scale, but understood almost nothing about the symbolism embodied in its structure and detail. It had very little meaning for one whose religious orientation was wholly outside Catholicism. I was, however, quite genuinely moved when I heard that their religion meant enough to the people of that time, both rich and poor, that they were willing to undertake extremely hard labor, pulling together to haul the great stones to the building site, so that the significant events and symbols of their faith could be preserved in stone. It was a labor of love, an expression of conviction and certainty, which I longed for, had never had, and still hoped to find. But this was not my way, and I had no wish to enter any further into it. Seeking is as much a process of rejecting and eliminating as it is of accepting and incorporating. The religious form expressed in Chartres left me cold and unmoved, but the fervor behind its coming into being gave me hope.

It was one of those exquisite summer days with which France can be blessed, when the sunlight is moderated and toned by a bluish haze, softening and harmonizing the elements of the landscape—when one feels a joy in the present and a nostalgia for the past in the same moment. For just then one is at peace with oneself and the world. Monet has caught this perfectly in his landscape, "Fields in Spring." It was such a day as we continued our journey south. We climbed and climbed, the old Pontiac chugging along and expressing its distress in its overheated engine. In spite of the slowness of our progress it wasn't a leisurely trip.

There were too many uncertainties. There was the car, the narrow mountain roads, which Mrs. Ripman was not used to driving, and a four year old, who was restless and wanted to be out and active. But there were also some wonderful surprises in that semi-alpine countryside. We stopped one evening just at dusk in a small village dating from the middle ages. The village residents had gone inside for their evening meal. As I walked along the narrow stone street, in the stillness and half-light of the evening I was transported back in time by the sights, sounds and smells. I could hear the murmur of voices on the upper floors of the houses, and the quiet chewing of the animals in the barn directly underneath, all under the same ancient stone roof. By now I had left my troubles and concerns behind in the enchantment of this beautiful country and its people and customs. In 1953 there were no overcrowded highways and hordes of tourists. France had almost recovered, and in the country they were hospitable and shared with us whatever they had in food. I remember at one small hotel someone was sent down to the brook to catch a trout for our four-year-old's supper, which of course delighted him.

Our climb did come to an end. We began our descent rather more easily, it seemed. At least the car was more willing. We were about to congratulate ourselves that we had made it, when at 1300 feet the brakes failed! Quick thinking on the part of Mrs. Ripman, who was driving, saved us. She simultaneously grabbed for the emergency brake and turned the car to the left into the mountain. We stopped with a jolt. She covered her face with her hands and wept. But we were all safe. Her husband, our Group Leader sitting next to her, said absolutely nothing throughout the whole ordeal, even after we stopped. I suppose he was remembering himself. We had come onto a beautiful mountain meadow, full of flowers, and our four year old could not wait to get out of the car and 'explore.' We were only a few hours from Grasse, our destination that day. The rest of the trip was made in silence laced with trepidation. By using the motor as a brake and the emergency brake judiciously we arrived safely. What burned me about this was the repair bill, which was $90.00, a significant sum in 1953, which as far as I know we were never reimbursed for by Dionne Lucas, nor was any apology made for the condition of the automobile. As I discovered, this was characteristic of the Work. One must not behave in 'the ordinary way' lest one stay in the rut one was in and not move on to a higher order of things. Later on, when I met Islam and the remarkable man who was to become our teacher, I was overwhelmed by the politeness and consideration he extended to us. It released emotions and feelings that had been so long held in check, and with the outpouring of them came a realization of how fragile was my stability and sanity, even though I had made strenuous efforts to "work on myself."

Naïve and still essentially a provincial, I was more than surprised by the French Riviera. It was a shock! I saw there more clearly how different the French are from us, and the differences were even more pronounced here in the south of France. In the USA in 1953 we had almost no nude bathing, except in a few isolated nudist camps. Public displays of affection were very limited. On the beach at Cannes there was endless fondling between couples lying stretched out on the sand. It was all rather harmless but far more excessive than was considered proper in America. The French women did not shave their under-arm hair. The men seemed to find this most attractive, and they ran their fingers through it and sniffed it, all accompanied by looks and sounds of pleasure. I saw Americans there who had gone native. My eyes really opened wide one day when as I was crossing the main street in Cannes I saw a very high-ranking official of the U.S. Government pull up in his very expensive sports car with his boyfriend beside him. They had stopped for a moment so the young man could go into a shop on the beach and visit a friend. I heard him say he would be only a minute as I walked around the car, which was obstructing what little traffic there was.

I didn't spend much time on the beach, tired as I was. I was too interested in exploring this fascinating area. There was the low road and the high road, and I took buses along both. My friends whom I had come with were, I soon discovered, more exhausted than I was. They could literally lie all day on the beach without speaking more than a few words to each other or to anyone else. I gleaned no gems of wisdom from either of them, even at dinner, which we sometimes ate together. If there were burning issues as to their identity and the meaning of life, they gave no sign of it. It was with relief and some fear that I set out alone for Italy. On the evening of my departure, while it was still quite light, they walked me down to the train, which was parked on the siding next to the through tracks, surrounded on both sides by lush fields of blooming flowers. There was no station, only the conductor to take my ticket. It wasn't a complete train, just a few cars to be hooked onto the main train, which was due any time. The three of them were standing at the window, the mother holding the boy up so he could see me off. When he discovered he was not going with me he struggled very hard to get out of her arms and into my window, screaming his protests. He made, as his father put it, "a hell of a fuss." Seeing his distress, I almost decided not to go. I wanted to stay but I couldn't see how I could help him. He was a dear child, and I was very fond of him. That separation broke the close relationship we had developed when I was staying with them. I later discovered this back in Vienna when, having asked him to do something, he informed me he would do only what his mother said to do, which was, after all, the right relationship. I got the message, even though it hurt.

I went on to Italy and to Capri, which I had wanted to visit from having read Axel Munthe's enchanting account of the place and its residents. It was still beautiful, but I could not see it through his eyes. One of my problems is to see the defects in people and places. My husband says I see the hole and not the doughnut. I am now able after many years to enjoy the virtues and attractiveness of places and people, observe their defects, record them and quickly pass over them. That is, unless the faults outweigh the virtues, and then the watchdog in me is very active. It's the kind of response one would expect from an adult whose childhood was full of threatening situations and negative responses, very hard to leave it behind. One's inner child is saying, "If I don't receive a loving response, I am at least prepared to fend off a blow." I had no quarrel with God's works on Capri or anywhere else, if they are unspoiled by man. What could be more satisfying than to gaze into the sapphire waters of the blue hole or to plunge into its crystal depths?

Alone now in Italy, my unease at my situation in Washington, returned. I had been able to put it aside at the beginning of this trip. It now returned. I was pretty sure that I was not going to improve unless I hired someone to help me. It was on the train back to Paris that I decided I must find an analyst. This was a sticky business, because I was employed by CIA, and I was sure they would consider it a security risk. I knew it wouldn't be, because I was dealing with the past. The fundamentals of it had nothing to do with what subject or area I was covering in the Agency. Moreover most of the information for our project came from unclassified sources. I simply didn't know any big secrets. So I went ahead and if the security boys knew it they never said anything to me. I just knew my need was great and that everyone would ultimately benefit from it. Having decided to do this, I was relieved, and in a burst of optimism and abandon I bought five or six hats in Paris. They were all very French, very stylish. I wore them for years afterward. One of them, an emerald green silk, I wore to the rehearsal dinner prior to our wedding.

As soon as I returned to Washington I called my psychoanalyst friend in Chicago and obtained the name of a practitioner in D.C. who would interview me and refer me to two analysts. I could then decide which one I wanted. I never interviewed the second one, and in some ways I think it was a mistake. The first one became my analyst. He was really all right in the beginning. I went twice a week and right away began to loosen up and be freer and more spontaneous. He looked very much like my father, although I did not consciously realize it until later. His mannerisms were also like my father in some ways. I went back to the Gurdjieff group meetings, but it was not the same. Mr. Ripman opposed the analysis, but everyone else, including Charles, thought it was a good idea. The Gurdjieff work's attitude to psychoanalysis came from Ouspensky's rejection of it. I'm not sure, but I think in England one was actually barred from coming to groups if one was undergoing psychoanalytical treatment.

A New Romance

Almost at once I began to feel better, especially about myself. I was also feeling hopeful. This analyst was the kind who made the patient do all the talking. For the first year he would just say, "uh huh," no matter many times he needed to intersperse it in my ramblings. I found it almost impossible to associate freely. Somehow we had not made contact, and the "uh huh's" were not reassuring enough for me. But I did become loose enough almost right away to communicate my feelings. I had not seen Charles since my trip. When he called me, asking if I could have dinner with him, my reply was totally uncharacteristic of me, unstudied, spontaneous, and frank. I said, "I would like to, but I never know how I am going to be these days. Why don't you come over, throw your hat in the door, and if it doesn't come sailing out, come on in." He was so intrigued by this approach, he later told me, he couldn't wait for the time to come. It was a very successful dinner. We went to the Shoreham Hotel's Sunday night buffet. It was a warm autumn evening and there was quite a crowd there because the buffets were good. It was an especially pleasing atmosphere. We had to park at the edge of the lawn. When we came out to our car, another had pulled in sideways and wedged us it. I looked the situation over and decided what he ought to do, but something told me to keep my mouth shut. I got in the car and sat quietly while he successfully manipulated his robin's egg blue Ford convertible out of this tight spot. The ground was soft and the car skewed around, making it even harder to extricate. Finally we were out, and on our way back to my apartment I had not said a word. He looked at me and smiled, but said nothing. I asked him if he would like to come in for a nightcap or a coffee. He quickly accepted. I put his coffee down on the table by his chair and sat down on the sofa. I looked at him without saying anything. His face lit up with a big smile and a look came over him as if someone had turned a light on inside him. He came and sat down on the sofa and took me in his arms and gave me a big hug and asked me to marry him! I was overwhelmed and so happy I could just nod yes. Later he announced that he always knew he would know the right one because the bells would ring. In that moment of the big smile on his face, the bells had rung.

We were married on January 16th, 1954, in the Unitarian Church by the Reverend E. Powell Davies. It was a rainy Saturday, but we didn't care for we were going to Haiti on our honeymoon quietly happy. Mr. Ripman had advised Charles not to marry me. It was too risky, he said, because no one could know how I would be after the analysis. But as with most things, Charles seeks the best advice he can find and then makes up his own mind. I was pretty shaky, because I wanted it to work, and I really didn't have much to go on to make it succeed, or at least I didn't think I had. My mother and sister came to the wedding, and my mother moaned that Charles was an only child and probably spoiled and would make me unhappy. I listened to this for a couple of days before the wedding, and then I sent her out to Vienna with the Ripman family. By now I had already changed enough not to put up with her moaning and gloom. I felt no guilt about it. My analyst approved the wedding and came to the reception. He took up his seat in a corner to observe all the exchanges. I noticed that even in a social situation he didn't communicate very well. Toward the end of my first year in analysis he had made in my opinion a fatal mistake in judgment. I had resigned from the Agency and was doing some freelance editing on a scientific conference. I missed one of my appointments with him because I had to review a paper with the author of one of the participants who was in Washington for only one day. The analyst didn't accept this excuse and was in fact very angry. He told me I couldn't do this to him, that I must keep my appointments. It was a replay of my past, not what I would have expected from a professional whose business it was to understand. As a result of this encounter, he lost me.

I continued to see him for another few months, but I was getting more help from Charles. I had one very bad weekend when my fantasies and my past just took over. I went through a series of imaginings and terrors that would last maybe for an hour, sometimes less. I remember one very clearly. We had by that time moved out to Vienna into a house we had commissioned to be built. It had windows all the way across the front of a large family room downstairs. I believe it was at the worst point of those two days that I sat there in the family room looking fearfully out and around one side of the house. I was sure there was a large spider out there just waiting to grab me and devour me. I remember Charles sitting there beside me holding my hands and telling me not to be afraid. I was a frightened five-year old. Afterward I referred to it as the lost weekend, but it wasn't that. Some things got worked out then and resolved and passed away. I never experienced anything like that again. I still don't know exactly what the event was, nor was the analyst of any help. Matters were so dark, and we were so distressed, that for the first (and the last) time in our lives we consulted the *I Ching*. Charles had a copy of Richard Wilhelm's translation of this ancient Chinese system of divination (Pantheon Books, 1950), and he decided we should consult it. We used the modern system of tossing three coins six times to construct the hexagram appropriate to our concern. The result was number 21 in the series, named *Shih Ho*, which means 'Biting Through.' At one point in the interpretations (p. 129) we read: "Bites on dried gristly meat. Receives metal arrows. It further instructs one to be mindful of difficulties and be persevering. Good fortune." That was enough for me, and we resolved to be patient and persevering, not allowing ourselves to think we had bitten off more than we could chew.

Sutton Island

In the summer of 1956 shortly before we moved to New York we were invited to visit our dear friends, the Rosenthals, in their beautiful old summerhouse on Sutton Island near Bar Harbor in Maine. We had all been in the Gurdjieff group in Washington and had become very good friends. Laurence was a composer and musician. They had driven from Altoona, PA, to Washington in a blinding snowstorm so that he could play the organ for our wedding two years before. After his military service during the Korean War they had moved to New York where there was work for composers. They had a little girl, age three, a gem of a child. His wife, Barbara, was pregnant with their second girl that summer. Neither Charles nor I will ever forget first setting foot on that wooded, moss-covered, enchanted spot that was Sutton Island. I'm sure there are many islands like this in that state so generously endowed with beauty that is Maine.

It was dusk on a warm evening in August when the mail boat from Southwest Harbor pulled up at the Harvard dock on Sutton and put us off on the float with our rucksacks and our Weimaraner, Gretchen. The island had only a dozen or so houses, no automobiles, and Charles was thrilled to see among the owners not only Harvard University, but Professor Goodwin, author of Charles' treasured Goodwin and Gulick Greek Grammar, and Hoyt Hottel, Professor of Chemical Engineering at MIT. The purity of the air and unspoiled beauty of the path we entered through an archway in the dense forest laid a spell over us, which lasted for fifteen years. In the winter we would dream longingly of the time when we could again walk its moss-covered paths and gaze into it's shaded forest glens. We actually did spend one Christmas there in 1964. On this first visit there, guided through the enchanted forest by our hostess, we came upon their handsome house beautifully sited on a rocky cliff above the sea. It had been built in the 1920's by William Burnham of Philadelphia, former Chairman of the Baldwin Locomotive Works. He had spared no expense in its construction. I don't mean that it was heavily decorated, but the woodwork and even the interiors of the closets were of superb workmanship. It was set on the north shore of the island, elevated perhaps twenty feet above the rocky coast. This was the stormy side of the island opening out to the ocean, and we used to say: "Look out there and you can see Spain!" It was a beautiful location in good weather and magnificent for viewing the ocean storms in bad weather. The house had two porches on the shore side, one open for good days, and one glass enclosed for bad weather. It had been allowed to run down, but it still had its beauty and was wonderfully suited for a family holiday with its large rooms and fireplaces. Most of the houses on the island were given loving names by their owners, and this one was known as Windermere.

In the fading light as we had approached their house we noticed a small log cabin about a hundred feet back from the shore almost smothered by the young fir trees which had grown up around it. It was a Hansel and Gretel cottage, and we expected at any moment that the "small folk" would peek out from behind the trees. We were still gasping at the beauty of the place when Barbara opened the door. We kept saying we did not know such a place still existed in this country. We asked about the cabin and learned that it was part of the property. Whether it could be purchased she did not know, but they were hoping to buy the main house in the near future. After two or three days there we were determined to own that cabin, called "The Dory" in recognition of its being a little vessel moored behind the big house. Set between the sea and the forest with its beautiful natural paths, and the birds and wild mink that fished off the rocks, it had us hooked.

The Rosenthals' next door neighbor was also from New York, a retired lawyer who loved the island as much as the rest of us. He also had an interest in seeing that congenial people bought property there and not "bums" as he called them, who would despoil the landscape with their lifestyle. After we went back to New York we talked to him and to the lawyers for the owners who lived in Philadelphia. Finally the matter reached the point that we could meet with the owners in Trenton, New Jersey. We were to meet them in the railway station, agree upon the price, and close the deal then and there. Carefully coached by our lawyer friend and soon-to-be neighbor, Mr. Chatfield, Charles took the train to Trenton. After surprisingly little back and forth, the owners agreed to sell the Dory and a specified piece of land around it for a thousand dollars. This was the spring of 1957, and we couldn't wait for July to come when we could start work on the cabin. It needed serious repairs. We had an electrician from Southwest Harbor rewire the place and install an electric hot water heater, stove and refrigerator. Charles spent most of that first summer under the cabin digging the rotted foundation beams out with a piton hammer. Next, using jacks he lifted the cabin enough to permit new beams to be inserted. One of the new beams was a great cedar which the island patriarch, George W. Paine of Boston allowed us to cut. We had it dragged by horse and sled to our property. Local laborers put on a new roof and new floor. The cedar shingles for the roof were delivered to the Southwest Harbor dock where they sat for a few days. Suddenly one foggy afternoon we heard a boat whistle off the Hessenbruch dock, the nearest to the Dory. Charles dashed down the path to discover Wilfred Bunker, the mail boatman, had the shingles (40 packages of them) which he tossed onto the dock with the explanation: "It's about to rain, and if they get all wet and heavy to carry, it's going to be your fault and not mine!"

The Dory consisted of one large room, 20' by 20', built of cedar logs from the island and originally intended to be the ice house for the Burnham house. A small addition had been attached which provided a tiny kitchen, closet, bath and extra bed. The big room's exposed cedar logs gave it a rosy tone, warm and agreeable. The fireplace in one corner was nearly eight feet wide with a mantle six feet long made of a single piece of island granite. The south wall had a window seat and a picture window of plate glass about five feet by four feet looking out onto what we called 'the fairy forest.' Nevertheless much of the undergrowth had to be trimmed and many trees felled to protect the cabin from damage from winter storms. We furnished the cabin with the excess from our Virginia house, and I made hand woven rugs for it in colors suitable for a forest house—dark, medium and light greens and warm reds and near purples to suggest the embers of the fireplace. For ten years the Dory was our escape from the stresses and strains of New York to which we were not at all naturally suited. When we sold it in 1969 for ten times what we paid for it, we were selling our blood, sweat, and tears as well as the ghosts of our ten years of pleasure in it. Thirty years later we visited the friends who bought it, and we were moved to see how little they had changed, including Charles's Alexander Calder-like chandelier made of paint cans suspended from the peak of the main room and his inscription carved in wood over the fireplace from Virgil's Eclogues: "Out of this wood do not desire to go."

Our vacation times in Maine were a kind of benchmark for us as to our progress and whatever change or improvement had taken place in our characters during the winter in New York, struggling with ourselves in the Gurdjieff Work, attending group meetings, doing physical work on Madame Ouspensky's farm near Mendham, New Jersey. The Dory and the island remained more or less the same, and we could recall each summer how we had been the previous summer. In a rough way we could tell whether we were getting anywhere. The change was agonizingly slow for all the effort we put into it and all of what I came to regard as the unnecessary nonsense one had to endure. It was purported to be a way of inner development, and supposedly it produced results, otherwise why would one make such efforts and give it so much time? But I saw people around me who had been trying for forty years and more, and I wondered what in the world they had been like at the time they entered "the System" as it was called and began "working on themselves." They seemed to me to have all the faults, flaws, and defects that I had and in some of them, a generous helping of arrogance as well. Added to this was the advantage of a certain power they exercised over the lives of others simply because of their seniority or that they had known Gurdjieff or Ouspensky. This was not always benign in its effect. Rather large groups working together in one location over several days or a week produce an energy to which some people are more sensitive and receptive than others. Individuals working in these groups need to be watched carefully by a leader who can recognize ill effects and know to intervene at the right moment. A person can be psychologically shattered and even months and years of therapy cannot put them together again. We saw and had to deal with several such cases during our years with the Work.

Anyone who has been fortunate enough to vacation in the more isolated areas of the Maine coast finds that time slows down, reminiscent of earlier eras of leisure. It was like this on Sutton. Once we had finished the restoration of the Dory, there were long days we could fill as we chose. Charles began to carve the native stone with different forms of calligraphy or studied Greek so that he could read the Gospels in the original. I walked the paths and explored the interior less trodden spots of the island. Together we hunted mushroom, of which we identified forty or fifty varieties to be found there, including two of the most poisonous, *amanita ascaris* and *the destroying angel*. When he was at the National Academy of Sciences Charles had known the Director of the New York Botanical Garden, Bill Robbins, and from him he obtained the recommendation of a book on "Mushrooms of the Eastern United States and Canada." Dr. Robbins thought this book was thorough enough to keep us from killing ourselves. On good days, after the sun was well up, we'd take our baskets and trowels and begin our search. There were several forms of chanterelles, boletus, cepes, proteus and many others. We were very careful about which ones we ate, trying to follow the experts on edibility and taste. We never got sick, but I wouldn't be so experimental now, simply because while a mushroom variety may be edible, it may also carry other fungi one may be allergic to. The island environment, almost always damp was favorable to the growth of a tremendous variety of fungi, some microscopic and many, I'm sure, unstudied and unidentified, so it is risky to eat even the edible ones. Living as I do in Rockland County, New York, also a high fungi area, there are times in mid and late summer when my eyes burn, I have some difficulty breathing, and I am unwell from a cause as yet undetectable by standard allergic tests. I say, it's not worth it to ingest wild mushrooms. Study them as interesting and beautiful forms of nature, but eat only the mushrooms you buy from the supermarket.

In summertime in Maine there may be two or three days of continuous rain. There may even be a wee bit of steady drizzle, a gentle dampness enough to discourage leisurely expeditions of discovery outside. When we knew enough about what to expect from the weather, we would save up our indoor hobbies for those days. Sometimes we would gather at the Rosenthals and listen to music or read poetry. Sometimes the Rosenthal girls would write and perform short plays. These pieces were often interesting and imaginative, even though the girls were quite young, five to ten or eleven years old. Sometimes it was just rainy and not stormy and we would all pile into the Rosenthals' Boston Whaler and go to Seal Harbor, tie up the boat. Walking a couple of miles through the woods we could go to the inn at Jordan Pond for afternoon tea, popovers, and homemade ice cream. Acadia National Park maintained this wild and beautiful structure with its huge fireplace in a generously scaled interior and rustic furnishings in the middle of an essentially wilderness area. There is always the danger of fire in such areas from carelessness, especially in extremely dry conditions with decaying organic matter and dead trees covering the forest floor. Several years after we left the island we heard that this fine old structure had burned to the ground.

The entire Rosenthal family, mother, father and the two girls, were very gifted either musically or artistically. We were often the beneficiaries of their talents in the form of small drawings or cleverly designed articles of beauty and utility. I still have and cherish a pair of toe stuffers from shoes made in the shape of a mouse, complete with ears, nose, eyes, and tail by Nadia, the oldest girl (who has gone on to become a world renown authority in biomedicine.) The younger girl, Maria, showed signs of becoming a writer, and although I no longer see them, I hear she has become a potter in England. I remember one especially memorable occasion on which Larry Rosenthal and the girls collaborated on a short musical composition to commemorate Charles's birthday. Larry composed the music for flute and recorder, and, sitting upright on their chairs in the Dory before a glowing fire, the girls played it. It was a touching moment, a mark of our relationship and fondness for each other.

It became a regular event to celebrate Charles's August birthday on the island. There wasn't any material thing he much wanted, but it pleased him enormously that I would go to all the trouble of preparing an elaborate dinner for the occasion. I started preparing for it several days ahead. Since there were no stores of any kind on the island, the food purchased in Southwest Harbor had to be brought to the island on the mail boat and wheel-barrowed to the cabin. I tried to make a real feast, using the fruit from the island if it was available—raspberries just outside our door, blueberries not far away, and the communal apple trees in the middle of the island behind "Afterglow" the house of the Hottels. One year I prepared a Persian dinner from memory and the help of a newly published Persian cookbook. There were sixteen dishes from appetizers to dessert. We always invited the residents at our end of the island and others we knew and liked to join in our feasts.

Island life was a peculiar phenomenon all its own. Almost every year there was some issue over which the residents could align themselves for or against each other, or against the local natives. There never seemed to be any neutrals, and the debates could get quite heated. There was something about being settled there on that little piece of heaven. Everyone had an intense wish to preserve the status quo. One year it was the water system. There was a fine well in the center of the island, which furnished the water for most of the island's ten or twelve houses. A family from Philadelphia, the Hessenbruchs, who had for three generations summered in their big house on two or three or possibly more acres in the center of the island owned the well. Although everybody was connected to the water system, since the well and pump were on the Hessenbruch property they maintained it. A time came when the head of the family died, and since his children were not interested in vacationing there, it fell upon the rest of us to take care of it. That summer, before all of us had appeared, there was great discussion and many proposals as to what we should do about the well. Everything was suggested from turning it over to the Town of Cranberry Isles, to trying to get the present owners, Princeton University to whom the house had been bequeathed, to continue maintenance.

One of the summer people, Jim Shaw, who was an investigator in the School of Dental Medicine of Harvard University, was also a good administrator and a practical man. He had heard about Mr. Hessenbruch's death in the winter and had alerted Charles that "we summer people" as the natives called us, might have to assume responsibility for the water system. So he and Charles had been thinking about the problem for a couple of months, and as soon as they both got to the island they discussed the options and called a meeting of the residents who used the water. They proposed the formation of a water company, with someone elected each year to administer it and hire a local man to inspect it periodically and actually do the work or repair and maintenance. It was highly amusing how soon the uproar died down once a feasible plan was presented and everyone had a chance to air his or her views at the meeting. The plan was accepted and the Sutton Island Water Company was formed with the help of a Southwest Harbor attorney. As far as I know, now some forty years later, it is still going. What a well!

Another year we discovered some new residents on the island, rabbits or I should say hares, immigrants from we knew not where. They certainly didn't swim there. We had pretty conclusive evidence that the local hunters brought them to the island in the winter, as hares had never been seen before. There were signs everywhere of their prodigious appetites, and they were not fussy about what they consumed. The island had some rare trees and plants, which all of us knew and protected as well as we could. We were no matches for the rabbits. The uproar became so heated that two or three of the people went to one of the mail boat captains to protest, knowing that he and his family were long time residents there and knew everything that went on. Of course, characteristically, he said little. However, the next year we could scarcely find a rabbit. Whether it was the hunters who rid us of them, or the wild mink who must have found wild hare a welcome change from fish and mussels, we never knew.

Those of us who had been there a few years and loved the island also understood how fragile its ecology was. Too many of anything coming from the outside, whether it be people or imported creatures, destroyed the precious balance. In the last three or four years we were there, increasing signs of depredation and change appeared everywhere. One would go for a walk on the main path and meet eight or ten people who were just "visiting" for an hour or two, having been brought over by the mail boatmen who could in this way add to their income from tourism. This would happen several times a day. We were getting too much publicity and too many stops were being made. The mail boats came as close to our shore as they dared so that the tourists could see the island's beauty, blasting forth its virtues over their sound systems. Several of the houses had been bequeathed to Universities, who allowed vacationing faculty members to use them for two weeks and perhaps never come again. They knew very little about the island and probably had no briefing beforehand. As a result branches of small rare pines would be torn off to grace the mantles of these houses, and rare wild-flowers were picked as though they were dandelions. I no longer dream about the island. It is truly in the past, but it was surely an enchanted interval in our busy and often hectic lives.

During our last summer on the island, 1971, we both felt that our time there was nearly over. Relationships had changed, especially with the Rosenthals. Larry was away composing a film score, and Barbara was alone with her two children. Charles couldn't get away for the whole month of August, and I was there alone for several weeks. Previous to that I often spent a morning or an afternoon with Barbara and the girls sitting on one of the porches, hunting mushrooms, or just visiting. That last summer was very different. They were away on their sailboat more, and when they were home Barbara seemed to be keeping her distance from me. I tried to discover what had caused the changed, but I was too unsuspecting then to see what was really happening. I knew their marriage wasn't good, and had not been for several years. I finally realized that Barbara was making her way into what might be called "society" with the summer people, especially the wealthy summer residents of Seal Harbor. These people had fine summer places, impressive boats, and membership in the very posh "Seal Harbor Club. They sailed, played tennis or golf, drank and partied. I'm not sure if she really liked them, but Barbara wanted to see what, if anything, was there and whether she would like it. She was young, lonely in a lot of ways, and very attractive. I think during this phase of her adventure she looked on me as rather too prim and judg-mental. She was certainly correct about both, but I did not judge her because I had nothing to judge. Charles and I drank very little and partied even less, and we found the people she was going around with to be dull and silly. I never had the opportunity to talk to her about her reasons for choosing this particular set.

The End of the Gurdjieff Work

Back in New York we all were busily involved in the Gurdjieff Work. I was over-seeing the weaving project at the Society for Experimental Studies at Armonk, the new place of work established after Madame Ouspensky died and her place at Franklin Farm near Mendham was sold. Barbara was involved in the Gurdjieff movements in Manhattan. We seldom met. Charles was jointly managing the construction of a new dining room added to the house at Armonk. It was to be large enough to hold 200 or more people for Sunday work. We were also at the Gurdjieff Foundation's building on 63rd street in New York one or two nights a week.

Actually Charles was there more often, about four nights a week, and I began to feel it was too much. In June of 1962 when the Foundation closed for the summer I began to examine my feelings. Was I being unreasonable or was he away too much and neglecting his home and me? We could never entertain friends anymore. We had no free evenings. Although ordinary social contacts among people in the Work were not forbidden, neither were they encouraged. I remember Madame Ouspensky's grandson, Lornia, a bachelor in his mid-forties living at Franklin Farm, came up to me one day and asked: "Why don't you ask me to dinner? I'll tell you some things about this place and the people here you ought to know." He was sharp tongued and had a rather difficult disposition so I wasn't too anxious to entertain him. I had the perfect excuse, which required no lie. I said that we didn't have any time to entertain anymore, and I was as sorry about it as anybody, but that was the way it was. That satisfied him, and he never asked me about it again.

I was also irritated by the way some of the old ladies who had known Gurdjieff and Ouspensky treated the rest of the women. The role of the mind was played down as if it was an impediment to spiritual development. We should *feel* more, in spite of the fact that Gurdjieff had said men should think less and feel more, and vice versa for women. These old ladies regarded the put-down as good for the soul. Although they hadn't a clue as to how to give real spiritual help, they had the art of the squelch down to perfection.

I was smoldering on several counts that spring when the Foundation finally closed and Charles and I at last had a free evening to talk. I began rather rationally and reasonably, but as I began to give the reasons of my distress I became further upset. I ended by flinging down an ultimatum: either Charles would devote more time to his home and to me or we would be finished. As I went on I saw that a stronger plea was necessary. I had rather feebly complained on one or two previous occasions with no positive results. I was already discontented with the Work. I had already had enough put-downs to last me for the rest of my life. I was very close to leaving it altogether. Only Charles's pleading with me to try a little longer kept me in the Work.

There was also our unsatisfactory relationship with our Group Leader, Louise Welch, who, with her husband, Bill Welch, shared our house on 84th Street in Manhattan. Charles and I had both knocked ourselves out to make the living arrangement work. If there was a plumbing leak in the basement or if their grandchildren plugged up the toilet it was we who cleaned up the sewage. If they forgot to take the plug out of the bathtub and it damaged the ceiling in our apartment we paid for the repair. If they forgot to shut off the water in the kitchen sink and their kitchen floor had three inches of water in it and it was running down into our kitchen light fixture, it was I who rushed up and mopped up their kitchen and then ours. Their credibility as people who could lead us toward enlightenment was shrinking with me every day. I felt like the little girl who said her only friends were books. My only friend at that point was my Weimaraner, Gretchen, and she was unhappy at being shut up in the apartment all day. If I left her alone she barked loudly and in that old house her bark went right through the ceiling to the Welch's apartment above. I felt this was not right, but I didn't know what to do about it. I left her with her veterinarian when we went to Armonk on Sundays, but during the week I had to leave her at home. In the spring of this dreadful year, just before we left for Maine, she came into season and hemorrhaged severely. I rushed her to the vet who stopped the bleeding and spayed her. Never in the eleven years of her life had she had this problem, and both the vet and I were puzzled by it. I brought her home, and in a few days we went off to Maine with her laid out on the back seat of the car. Charles carried her from the car all the way to the boat and up to our cabin on the island. She laid on the window seat on a heating pad for several days until she was able to walk. Little by little she could get around the island, which she also loved.

I hadn't solved the problem of her barking, but I had a reprieve from dealing with it and the whole situation of our neighbors while we were in Maine. When we returned to New York City in the fall I wanted to get her out for walks, but she was a big dog and the pressure on my varicosed legs from her pulling on her leash was too painful. I had to let her do her bowel movements on the concrete behind the house. I didn't always get it promptly cleaned up. I regretted this neglect and the unpleasant sight to the neighbors, but it was an indication of my failing state of health and my depressed psychological condition that I could no longer fulfill my many commitments. Not only was my health failing, but I was also miserable about my life. It was sapping my energy and my attention. Here I was, caught in another unpleasant no-win situation, roiling early feelings that my mother could care for our dogs better than I could. Now the authority figure was not my mother, but our Group Leader, Louise Welch, who was suffering from our dog's barking. Where was the love hoped for? It was a cycle that repeated itself over and over, even though I was trying every way I knew to break it. I realize now that I clung to that dog because losing her would mean a loss, beyond doubt, of a big source of love.

Mrs. Welch, like my mother, in countless little ways, tore at my frail self-image. She affirmed what furthered her efforts to be a Group Leader and to carry out what she thought was the method for helping others toward self-realization. Thus does the ego in its quest for dominance destroy whatever thwarts it. One of the original Russian group, Mme. deHartmann, who had accompanied Mr. Gurdjieff on his famous trek across the Caucasus expressed it to us later: "Mr. Gurdjieff could knock you down but catch you before you hit the ground. These people only know how to knock you down, but they don't know how to catch you." The experience was like a horrible nightmare, which wouldn't go away.

So when we returned to New York in September, nothing had changed. I still hadn't found a solution to the problem with the dog, and I couldn't bear the thought of giving her away. No one said anything more to me about it, but one day when I let her out in the back yard I noticed a white pill on the concrete, which I picked up before she could eat it. I started staying with her when she went out, but one day in October she picked up another white tablet and swallowed it before I could get to her. When we went inside after about fifteen minutes she began to retch but couldn't vomit. She swelled up in just a few minutes. I quickly put on her collar and leash and rushed her in a taxi to the vet who was twenty blocks away. I'll never forget that ride. The driver was afraid she was going to be sick in his cab, the traffic was heavy, and she was suffering. Finally we got to the vet's office and after examining her he said he would try to pump her stomach. I couldn't bear to watch that, and since I trusted him, I left her in his care. Charles was at a Heart Association meeting in Atlantic City. I called him, but neither of us could do anything more. The next morning the vet called and said he had bad news for me. I knew at once that Gretchen was dead. I was too shocked to cry and I couldn't stand to be alone in that apartment. I called Charles from his meeting and he started home as quickly as he could. I got dressed and went out and walked and walked and walked until it was time for Charles to be home. Late that afternoon we picked up Gretchen's body, wrapped her in a blanket, and took her to the Rosenthal's home in the country where we buried her in their back yard. That was in October 1962. I was finally able to cry, and I cried off and on for the next six months. I cried so much I was sore in my chest and ribs. Not long after that, in late 1963 or early 1964 I began to have dreadful attacks of nausea and pain so severe that only Demerol would stop them. I had many tests, but no one seemed to know what the trouble was. Since the attacks usually started after a meal or sometimes if I ate only a small bit of something. I went on a diet of practically no fat and small meals. Until then I had always been strong and healthy. Now I was seriously ill.

One night when Charles was at the Foundation and I was feeling at the end of everything, I sank down onto the floor beside our bed and wept. I hadn't prayed in years, but I realized that this was all that was left. I pulled myself up and resting on my knees as I was taught as a child, I prayed for help. I didn't ask for anything specific, just for help. It was a long time coming, but for a life like mine it's a miracle that it could be turned around at all in the time that was left to me. I was almost fifty, seriously ill, and utterly discouraged.

In spite of the condition of my health I managed to do fairly well what was necessary in our apartment and to conduct the weaving sessions at Armonk and in my basement loom room. It was a big effort, and as far as I could tell not much was happening. No one took up weaving seriously. Most of the women I was working with had such personal problems that they were unable to undertake any project, which required study and effort. I remember at Armonk one of the regulars among the young women talked more than she worked, and I couldn't stop her. She had difficulty approaching and completing tasks in her ordinary life. She was a housewife with two children and a husband in advertising. The breakfast dishes would sit in the sink all day, and the children's dirty diapers would lie in a heap on the floor. She functioned mostly in her head, and in my opinion she not only disliked the role of mother and housewife, but she was unsuited for it, even though she loved her children and tried to care for them. She and her husband were in a younger group under our Group Leader, who had talked to her about this. She knew it was not good, but she couldn't change it. Her husband was losing patience with her and interest in her. She needed a kind of help the Gurdjieff Work couldn't provide nor could any of the rest of us. Finally Mrs. Welch advised her husband to divorce her, which I found to be appalling, and only added another wrong, considering the two children. This was only one of several situations in which the Group Leaders, among whom the Welches were certainly more enlightened than the rest, seemed to be totally ignorant of the advances in psychology and social enlightenment whose tools were available and could have been tried. I suppose it was a hangover from Ouspensky's attitude, for he was deeply suspicious of psychiatry. I have mentioned earlier the energies that were generated during some of our Work periods of a few days or a week, first at Mendham and later at Armonk, and how some couldn't handle them. I know personally of two cases at Armonk, both young men in their early thirties and regulars at the Sunday Work sessions. I was there one day when one young man began hallucinating. His Group Leader quickly washed his hands of it and told some of the senior members in his group to take him away. They managed to get him back to his family in Pennsylvania after a horrendous two days of trying to calm him down. He was ill for months afterward, and I think he was institutionalized. The other case occurred after we had left the Gurdjieff Work. We became acquainted with him when a good and devoted friend of his brought him to our house for lunch. He was in a pitiable condition, heavily medicated, and while he smiled pleasantly, he was unable to say a word. His friend brought him because he hoped we knew how to help him. We took him to our Spiritual Master of whom I will write below, and he received help to become a functioning human being again.

One of the most important activities in the Gurdjieff Work was something called the Movements or sometimes Sacred Dances. Gurdjieff claimed he had seen the notations for them in a monastery or religious retreat somewhere in the Middle East or Central Asia. He had worked them out and used them in his teaching methods. When he died he left instructions with his spiritual heir,

Madame Jeanne deSaltzman, who had been a dancer with the Dalcroze System in Russia and understood body movements. Under her the Movements classes had become an essential part of the Gurdjieff Work. They were complicated movements to music accompanied by mental exercises such as remembering numerical sequences based on the strange repeating decimals of the fraction one-seventh: 0.14285714285714...and so on to infinity. They had been performed in Paris and America for many years. Their purpose was training in controlling attention and observing one's reactions. Performing these repeatedly for several minutes or a half hour had the effect of changing the psychological state of people in the class. At least that was their intention, but for me they were so difficult that I felt at the end of a class as if I had been on a torture rack. Any elevation of my state was from the relief from being able to stop.

In 1963 Madame deSaltzman decided it was time to give a public demonstration of the movements in New York, which was an extraordinary undertaking. Work on this project extended over the fall and winter. I had persuaded my mother to spend that winter with us in New York rather than remaining alone in her home in Ohio. I was doing some of the sewing on the costumes for the demonstration and redoing some of the botched efforts of people who knew nothing about sewing. One of the beliefs of the Work was that people should, by control and application of their attention, be able quickly to learn and use skills and crafts—an ideal seldom realized. Even though her central vision was gone by then, Mother was helping me, because she knew a great deal about working with cloth. Expensive fabrics were being used, mostly Thai silks, and the patterns were created by following the designs and instructions in Tilke's series on *Costume Designs and Patterns.* I enjoyed this work and was left pretty much alone because none of the Group Leaders or their workers knew much about sewing. Sometimes I worked at home with Mother because she wasn't allowed to come to the Foundation. This was to be a big event, staged in the Fashion Institute of Technology's theater, and Mme deSaltzman had persuaded the noted theatrical producer, Peter Brook, who was in the Work in England, to do the staging. After endless rehearsals, and in order to polish people's performances, some of the Paris group came to work with the New York classes. Only the advanced New York pupils took part with a few of the younger members who were considered to be very good at the movements.

The reviews by the public were mixed, some obviously having no understanding of what the movements were all about. We were criticized for not preparing the audience with more information about their source and purpose. One movement, called "The Trembling Dervish," was performed by a group of men moving with great restraint and precision in a circle while a lone dancer, the trembling dervish, hopped about in the center in a spastic and insane manner from one foot to the other. The effort for the trembling dervish was great, and of course he had been rehearsing it for a long time before the performance. A short time later he appeared at the door of the Foundation with an axe, quite mad, demanding to see the head of the Foundation whom he intended to kill!

Charles was assigned the task of Lighting Engineer for Peter Brook, who was the "producer" of the event under Mme deSaltzman. He found this task fascinating. It was a good (and rather successful) example of the principle that Gurdjieff people should be able quickly to learn new skills. Having never had any experience with theatrical productions, Charles had to meet with Peter in his hotel the night of his arrival and take notes as Peter went through the program and described the lighting effects he wanted for each movement. Then he had to go to the Fashion Institute and figure out how to program the complex computerized lighting control system and be ready for the first dress rehearsal the next day. At the end of the performance Mother and I were standing at the back of the auditorium waiting for Charles to join us from his lighting control booth in the top of the auditorium. As we stood there three of the old ladies who 'manned' Mendham (I use the term advisedly) entered the lobby. As they passed by I introduced my mother to them. They gave no sign that they had heard me. My mother then thinking they did not hear me introduced herself and told them she had worked on the costumes. They passed on without so much as a nod. As you can imagine, this added to my examples of unnatural behavior by the Gurdjieff people. Why in the name of heaven did I remain 18 years in such a system? Nonaffirmation and psychological stress had become my way of life, coupled with a ridiculous optimism. Anyone knowing my history would say that I had not given up finding love hoped for.

In working with other people at the Foundation and at Armonk I tried to be kind and considerate to everyone. I know there were some who thought I did not understand what the Work was about and that I was really a fool. I had had to swallow so much venom myself and knew what it had done to me, I simply could not inflict that on others, even though their efforts at physical work were often inept and clumsy. I tried to affirm what was good and undamaged and hoped that they would find help for the other sides of themselves. It is hard to believe from this account that I was generally cheerful and had good friends in our group and in other groups. Both Charles and I sometimes doubled over in laughter when we got home at something that had happened at Armonk or the Foundation. Once we were laughing hilariously when our Group Leader, Louise Welch, and her husband returned from the Foundation and heard us as they passed our door. Dr. Welch, who often bridled at the mock solemnity that seemed to accompany the Work, knocked on our door, and when we opened it he gasped sarcastically, "Did I hear laughter?" Then he repeated it slowly, "Laughter?" as if it was an unheard-of event. It's one of my blessings that I have sometimes been observant and perceptive enough to see the humor and absurdities in the behavior of others (and myself), and we laughed with Dr. Welch.

Mrs. Welch also led a group in Canada which she visited from time to time, and individual members came to New York for consultation with her. She decided to have a week of intensive work there and wanted several of her New York group to participate. It was to be held on the farm of one of the Canadians. Since I was not well there was a question whether I should go. It was finally decided that I could go if I adhered strictly to my diet. I discovered at our first meal that no one had told the Canadians about my restricted diet. There was almost nothing at the first meal there that I could eat so I filled up on bread. They were apologetic and quite willing to prepare food for me that I could eat once they were informed of my situation. It was not a good beginning, but I soon forgot about it because I was busy and I liked the Canadians. They hadn't learned to tramp on others' toes yet.

We had another such session at Mendham shortly after Mme Ouspensky's death and before it closed. Charles was not feeling too well, and it was actually the beginning of a long period of being unwell. At the morning break for coffee on the first day at Mendham he felt faint and very tired. It was thought that it might be a hypoglycemic reaction. Eating a small amount of food would sometimes help but this condition plagued him for the next ten years. Our physician discovered the cause of the difficulty through a series of tests at New York University Hospital (a rare problem of bio-unavailability of glucagon which recovers blood sugar stored in the liver). Various remedies didn't help him. Periodically, from a few days to a few weeks, he would waken with a severe lack of energy. Pushing with all the will he could muster he would get through the day and come home to sleep for several hours. Usually by the next day he would recover. He was not cured until Sheikh Fadhlollah Haeri, a friend from the Middle East, who was aware of this problem, provided real help. On a pretext of requesting hospitality for one of his associates, he sent Dr. Qasem, a homeopath from India, to stay a weekend with us. Dr. Qasem talked with Charles in depth and after many questions prescribed a well known homeopathic medication in very high strength. He warned that if successful, the medicine would cause a "healing crisis" marked with breaking-out of the skin. After a few weeks the healing crisis occurred, which in the absence of Dr. Qasem's warning would have sent Charles to a dermatologist. Soon thereafter the problem disappeared and has never returned.

Along with everything else we did in the Work, Mme de Saltzman instructed the Group leaders to begin to study various religions and traditions. Some chose Christianity, some Judaism, others, Islam, Buddhism, the Greek myths, etc. I chose the Odyssey and Charles chose Islam. The idea was to study these sources carefully to see if we could find similar ideas to those expressed by Mr. Gurdjieff. Whether it was to confirm them as coming from authentic historical philosophical and religious sources or to clarify the real nature of his ideas by seeing them expressed in different forms throughout the ages no one ever said. Mme de Saltzman from time to time suggested these studies perhaps came from instructions left by Mr. Gurdjieff. It might have been to give a new impulse to our work and to keep our interest. These details never reached us, the classless trainees at the bottom of the pecking order. Periodically we would meet with others and exchange what we had learned. This made it possible for each of us to know at least something about each one of these areas. I remember very clearly Charles's presentation of his material on Islam one night at Franklin Farm in New Jersey. He did something I had never seen him do. To illustrate a point he was making he opened the Qur'an, in translation of course, and began to read. For some reason not even clear to him today, he began to weep, and for several minutes he was unable to continue.

Around the time that we were working on these studies, Mme de Saltzman presented another idea to Group I. This group consisted of those who had known Mr. Gurdjieff and were the only ones considered to be members of the Foundation. Under Mme de Saltzman's direction they were like a Board of Overseers who put into effect and guided the policies of the Work in America. Another group was designated as Group II, consisting of those somewhat less in seniority. Then at the level of Group III were several groups like our own who were under the various Group I members. As far as I could tell this had nothing to do with the status of one's spiritual progress. From the top down the groups had a mix of those who understood something and tried to live it as they understood it, and others of like seniority whose being and character and behavior showed no trace of anything spiritual, or even ethical, having ever touched them. Quite the contrary, their private lives were shameful and they lacked even a millimicron of conscience. They reminded me of the cartoon in the New Yorker of new arrivals in hell being told: "There's no right or wrong here, just whatever works for you."

On one of her annual visits in the latter part of 1961 or early 1962 Mme de Saltzman presented an idea for the New York people to undertake. We were to research and try to put together all the elements of an "Oriental Street" which we would then construct and furnish with all the items that would make such a place a functioning reality. This meant shops, articles for sale, costumes for the merchants and customers, places where craft articles were manufactured, authentic ornamentation such as calligraphy, and preparation and sale of food. Oriental dances and music were to be presented as well as traditional story telling. Mr. Gurdjieff in his writings had described such places, people and customs in such a fascinating way as to produce a nostalgia in the reader as if this places and people were the real home of all of us. At least this is the way it affected some of us.

For Charles and me, it stirred up a longing to visit that part of the world. With others he also began to study Arabic and Persian calligraphy. The goal of their work was to be a large plaster piece over a gateway with a chapter from the Qur'an in Arabic written or carved upon it. Other smaller pieces of calligraphy were also produced. Much time and research went into learning how to prepare the traditional ink based on recipe's discovered in mediaeval sources. Charles even gained access to the Arabic and Persian archives of the Metropolitan Museum (through the secretary of the Curator of the Near East Division who was in the Work) in order to study the sequence of strokes in writing various styles. Several of the women, including me, began to search the shops of Manhattan for materials necessary for the preparation of Middle Eastern and Oriental food. A group of us would prepare several dishes and try them out on any volunteers we found. We looked to help from anyone who had been in that part of the world or who knew exotic food. Today many good oriental cookbooks are available; then we were overjoyed when we found just one Persian, which was authentic.

I was also studying Oriental carpets and had purchased a number of books about them. While this was useful for the Oriental Street project, I had already begun studying carpet design. I had heard that there was religious and mystical symbolism in some of them. It was implied that understanding this symbolism would unlock some esoteric secrets. I saw clearly that there were symbols in them, but I never found them to be carriers of living ideas. In some of us is the desire to find an authentic living purveyor of the power of God and to experience it directly. It may be dormant in most and overlaid with disillusion and unbelief to an extent that higher influences cannot reach them. But for those who are actively looking for the evidence of God on this earth, these works of art containing such symbols may arouse that sleeping wish and guide them to the religious form that satisfies the seeker's need. Several women in our group studied the motifs and designs of oriental carpets in this way. We even traced them in detail to see whether we could fathom meaning or symbol. I used to work six or seven hours at a time in this way, re-drawing the more complicated and, I thought, most beautiful patterns. Some of them took on a three-dimensional perspective. It seemed to me there was so much life in them that they might begin to move.

We studied these subjects and objects in detail, which we might never have done except under that often irritating, but in this case effective way called the Work. It led some of us in directions I doubt we could have found by ourselves or followed thereafter. These studies must have been a part of the legacy from Mr. Gurdjieff to Madame de Saltzman. He may have thought they would create a longing to know better the culture which made possible the creation of these articles of beauty. Although she, herself, may not have fully grasped their purpose, Madame deSaltzman was conscientiously trying to carry them out. The Oriental Street was never realized because on the day on which it was to have first been presented, President Kennedy was assassinated. The project was cancelled and never revived, but some of us had made sufficient acquaintance with another world to want to experience it firsthand.

Iran and a New Adventure

It took a year or more for this impulse to push us into action, strengthened by our growing dissatisfaction with the Work. We had never seriously and actively thought of withdrawing. We were reluctant to do so because we had both invested so much time and effort to it. We had not lost hope that there might be something worth knowing not yet disclosed. Each year when the Foundation closed for the summer, and we had not found or had the secret revealed to us, we would say to each other: "Maybe next year. Maybe next year they will tell us what we want to know." At the same time we continued to want to see for ourselves the carpets and the architecture and the culture of their origin. Looking at a map of the Middle East, Turkey, Morocco, Egypt, Iraq and Iran we went over in our minds all that we knew and decided the place to go was Iran. They had some beautiful, relatively intact architectural monuments. They certainly had the best carpets and carpet industry. A book by Roger Stevens, former British ambassador to Iran, reinforced our decision: *Land of the Great Sophy*. Stevens was trained in architecture, and he described many sites off the beaten path, including the beautiful tomb of a Sufi Saint, Shah Ni'matullah. Unlike many of the tombs this Saint's tomb was being well cared for, which gave us reason to believe we might find something interesting there.

Charles says that by himself he would never have gone to Iran if I had not proposed it. But once we had decided to go both of us started collecting all the information we could find, asking whoever might have traveled there, reading all books relevant to this part of the world even Middle Eastern titles even though not specifically about Iran. We acquired a lot of information in this way about a country that in 1965 was little known and even less visited. We were also given contradictory and confusing advice. One friend arranged a lunch for us with a native who strongly advised us against making the trip because we would surely be attacked by bandits. Only at the end of the lunch we discovered that our well-meaning friend didn't know the difference between Iran and Iraq. The Iraqi whom we met had never been in Iran. Others would tell us that all our fears were nonsense. As one person put it: "You are going to the cradle of civilization."

Enthusiasm for the trip overcame my husband's distaste for travel. In early August 1965, having flown 8,000 miles, tired but alive with anticipation, we were passing over the desert of Iraq and could see nomad's campfires punctuating the darkness. Then soon after we saw the amber globes of Teheran's street lamps as we circled to land at Mehrabad Airport ("Abode of Kindness" in Farsi).

We had entered another world, very old and far stranger than anything we had anticipated, but not unfriendly. In those early post-World War II years there was a large fund of good will toward the United States. We had helped them over some hard times. Truman had been firm enough with Stalin to get him to pull his troops back out of Iran and into Soviet Azerbaijan or risk confrontation with us. We were the recipients of that goodwill wherever we went as soon as they found out we were Americans.

We had come just in time to see some of the old Iran. The Shah's modernization program, or as he called "The White Revolution" had hardly started. After about twelve hours sleep we stepped out into a glorious Persian morning. In our rented Volkswagen bug (chosen because of its air-cooled engine for a desert environment) we found our way to the edge of the city and the road south to Shiraz and Persepolis, the palace that Alexander the Great had sacked and burned. The unpaved streets at the edge of the city were overflowing with all manner of vehicles and pedestrians—women in black chodors, the tent-like outer covering worn by many women as they did their shopping or go to the mosque; carts or small wagons with large wheels drawn by horses long past their prime, some barely able to walk, but nevertheless urged on by impatient drivers; shepherds herding their wandering sheep and goats along the side of the road. Others both men and women were running for an ancient and already overloaded bus which sat belching its smelly fumes. Coffee-skinned, turbaned old men in baggy trousers carried bundles of fresh greens, their backs bent by the heavy loads. Rugs were laid out at the edge of the road to be "antiqued" by the wheels and feet that ran over them. Pigeons swiftly alighted in the midst of all this chaos and with practiced aim grabbed some morsel of food and just as quickly flew off again. Emaciated dogs, noses to the ground, hunted along the roadside for anything they could possibly eat. Aproned waiters deftly balanced their trays filled with small glasses of tea as they trotted along to their impatient customers. Spotted here and there in this moving mass were donkeys placidly keeping to their accustomed pace, indifferent to the urgings of their driver. We drove slowly (for there was no other way) through this incredible jumble of men, machines, and beasts. In spite of its composition a certain order permitted a slow movement. This early morning maneuver was our introduction to Iran. It was the beginning of a journey strange, pleasing and exciting, but at the same time it was like coming home.

Sufism

The other journey, begun on a later trip to this fascinating and often mysterious country, was a journey of the heart. Thirty-five years later it is not yet finished. Some said we were very courageous to have undertaken the first trip at all. We knew how essentially timid we were. We tried our best not to offend the citizens of our host country. At the same time, we were looking, looking, looking. We might be examining the beautiful carpets in the rug bazaar or standing silently in the mosques while the people were at prayer. Wherever we went we were looking for some sign, moved by some unspoken conviction that what we had been searching for so long was here. We had sat at home with our maps and all our marshaled information about esotericism, political climates favorable to it, and as much history as we could find about its migration. In the early 60's there was still very little published material available. Idris Shah had not yet brought out his series of books, beginning with *The Sufis*. We had not yet found the more scholarly books in the Oriental Division of the New York Public Library, most of which were in Farsi and therefore inaccessible to us.

Finally we obtained some definitive information from Hugh Ripman, our first leader in the Gurdjieff Work in Washington. He had traveled all over the world for the World Bank and Monetary Fund and had made it a practice to try to find any holy men whenever he went on business to the Middle East or the Far East. We were planning a second trip to Iran in the summer of 1966, but we could not yet admit to ourselves or anyone else that we were really looking for more than we had in the way of spiritual guidance. So we told Mr. Ripman (and ourselves) that we thought it would be good to meet some individuals following other "Ways" and hear from them of their experience. In spite of the fact that we had left his group in Washington to go to New York where we thought we would find a more complete form of the Work, he graciously provided us with information we would otherwise have spent years to obtain. Most importantly, he gave us a letter of introduction to the retired Chairman of the National Iranian/American Oil Company, Abdullah Entezam, who, he said, would take us to one of the Holy men he had met in Iran. Others have found teachers, but often only after sitting in cafes and tea shops and wandering through the bazaars of the Middle East for years. We were fortunate to have made a direct contact, and although Mr. Entezam's address had changed, he was so well known that the desk clerk in our hotel quickly tracked him down for us.

We hadn't been mistaken about our attraction to Iran. We realized how happy and excited we were to be here again as we sat having our bread and cheese and yogurt breakfast on the balcony of our room in the Park Hotel. People are up and about their business by 7:30 in the morning in the Islamic countries, even earlier they are abroad for the Morning Prayer in the mosques. The shops are open, the bakers are turning out their freshly baked slabs of bread and lines are forming to buy it. Deliverymen pedal along on bicycles balancing a stack of them on their handlebars. There was new construction all over Teheran. Old houses were being torn down and replaced by office building; new hotels were being built. The pace had quickened even in the year since our first visit. Change was blowing over this desert country, and, as always, not all of it was good.

We knew better this time why we were here. We had seen the carpets, the calligraphy, the ruins, the mosques, the palaces and the jewels on our first trip. These were temporal edifices inspired and built by ideas that were timeless, indestructible, and as alive in the 20th century as they had been at their emergence thirteen hundred years before. The challenge was to find that one who understood them, their living relevance, and could convey it directly and unequivocally to us, who understood very little about them and who had spent our lives entirely outside their tradition. The problem was not only one of transmission, but also our ability to recognize such a person once we were in his presence. This latter concern was not crucial, however, as later events showed us so clearly.

As soon as we could arrange it we went to the apartment of Mr. Entezam with our letter of introduction. By Iranian standards his dwelling was exceptionally modest for a man who had held such high positions (he had been one of the Iranian delegation to the United Nations Organization conference in San Francisco in 1948). Only one servant, an old woman, was in evidence. He welcomed us cordially and motioned us to seats in a small sitting room. It was a hot summer day and the sherbet and melon the old woman brought us was equally welcoming. He read our letter and smiled. Yes, he remembered our Washington friend, and he would be glad to take us to meet His Holiness, Pir Naseralishah, who was at present out of town. He suggested that in the meantime we go to Isfahan and

Shiraz, do our sightseeing, and on our return he would take us to meet him. He also suggested we see someone in Isfahan, an old man whom he knew well, and who we learned was a Sheikh in one of the principle Sufi orders in Iran. In the Arabic orders and in Sunni Islam the head of an order is called a Sheikh, and his helpers are called a "moghadam." In Iranian esotericism and Shia Islam, the head of an order is called a "Pir" meaning "elder" and his assistants are called Sheikhs. Also the term "Irfan" (Gnosis) is preferred among the Shias to "Sufism." Our letter of introduction was for the purpose of meeting with the Pir of the order of dervishes to which Mr. Entezam belonged (and into which we eventually learned our Group Leader in Washington had been initiated). After a pleasant hour with this agreeable and intelligent man, we returned to our hotel and prepared to drive to Isfahan the next day.

I don't know how it is today, but in 1966 many more of the old practices and attitudes remained in Isfahan than in Teheran, the capital of Iran which had seen and copied much of western styles and practices. In the bazaar in Isfahan we were amused to see a Mullah trying to greet one of his flock, but to do so he had to look at me, walking alongside the person he wanted to greet. To avoid looking at me, a woman and a western unbeliever besides, he turned his head to one side and at the same time waved a greeting to his friend. It was also in Isfahan that a young woman loudly criticized my outfit, which I thought was quite modest. The next year this same woman turned and shoved me rudely from behind as we passed on the street, although I was dressed even more modestly. Just at the beginning of the Islamic Revolution in 1979 a young woman convert to Shia Islam who had taught English to Iranian Children in Isfahan told me her story. When the trouble started there she went to the chief Mullah dressed in her chodor. She introduced herself in Farsi, told him how she was employed, and begged him not to firebomb her house. Two nights later they did just that. She not only left Iran, but she also almost lost her faith. When I met her, two or three months after this, she was still trying to reconcile what had happened to her in Isfahan with the Islam she thought she knew and had accepted as her religion. She was staying with some understanding and educated Muslim friends. With their help she had been able to resume saying her prayers, but she refused to wear the chodor, which was to her a symbol of all that was wrong with what was happening in Iran.

The small animosities I noticed in pre-revolutionary Isfahan were, fortunately for us, minor compared to the hospitality and kindness extended when people learned that we were interested in learning about Islam. The shopkeepers in the bazaar, the caretakers in the mosques, the taxi drivers, and hotel clerks, all graciously and patiently answered our questions. Islam advises us to judge people by their intentions, not their actions, and that is what everyone we had any dealings with seemed to be doing. It was the same when we visited the Sheikh Mr. Entezam had suggested we meet. His house was at the intersection of two old and narrow streets so characteristic of the Middle East. They are more like the alleys that run behind the houses in some of our cities. Nothing of the house was visible from the street, but once inside the gate, we saw a large yard and a platform where carpets were spread out for guests to sit on warm days drinking tea and eating fruit. We were greeted by a young boy whose English was rather good, whom we later learned was the Sheikh's grandson. He motioned us to go inside and we entered a large room where we found an old man sitting on the floor. He invited us to sit down in front of him. He was smoking a *narghile* (bubble-pipe) filled with water, but no tobacco. He explained to us that the moist air was good for his ailing lungs. I tried to observe him without staring, and I noticed how impassive and peaceful his face was. He answered our questions, which Charles put to him in his meager and stumbling Farsi. The Sheikh was neither judgmental nor overly eager to please us. He simply sat quietly and smiled a little from time to time. It was a pleasant meeting, and we left feeling that we had met a benign and good individual. Charles expressed our thanks and he replied that he thanked us for coming, saying: "You have asked me questions about God and it makes me happy to talk about God." Nevertheless we were not overwhelmed by his presence.

We continued on to Shiraz as we had planned. The road descends into the city down a hill, and at the edge of the city passes through an ornamental gate. Later we stopped at the gate to climb up its narrow stair and enter a small room over the road in which is a huge Qur'an, which the Shirazi's consider to be the guardian of their city. We enjoyed the peaceful air of Shiraz, scented with orange blossoms. We visited the Tomb of the poet, Hafiz, again. I am not a tomb visitor, and it was only because of his sublime poetry and the descriptions I had from others that I was interested in going. The people have such awe of Hafiz that they go to his tomb for divination. It is in the center of a garden, around the edge of which are other tombs with inscribed stones flat on the earth as is the custom in Islam. Hafiz's tomb, however, is a small elevated circle covered by a copper dome in the center of the garden. Seekers go up the two or three steps to the tomb and open a book of Hafiz's poems at random while bearing their question in mind, and from what they read they interpret the answer to their question. Tombs and cemeteries are quiet places, and they may be the only silent sanctuaries left to us as we approach the 21st century and its noisy machines.

The tomb of another famous Persian poet, Sheikh Saadi, is also in Shiraz. Although the he is buried in his garden, which is old, the tomb is a rather imposing structure of modern design. A river flows beneath the garden, reminiscent of an oft-repeated phrase in the Qur'an describing paradise: "Gardens beneath which rivers flow." A circular opening with a spiral stair leads down a few feet to a hole cut in the earth where one can see the rapidly flowing stream in which blind fish swim and snatch bread crumbs visitors throw to them.

In Shiraz we considered whether to re-visit the Sheikh when we returned through Isfahan, but neither of us wanted to see him again. Only later did we understand why. It was time to return to Teheran. We returned by the old road through Saveh, just because we had not seen the area west of Teheran on our previous visit. It was mostly desert with a few small villages and a lot of what we Midwesterners called "washboard road." Instead of the modern asphalted main highway the roads were the local terra firma with a layer of gravel, which packs down into the mud in the wet season, making a good surface if properly maintained by periodically scraping and evening the surface. However, more often than not, the road grader's pressure is uneven or its blade is misaligned and the irregularities it leaves are exacerbated by the traffic until the entire surface is like a washboard. In Ohio and on Michigan gravel roads we learned how to drive on such surfaces without being shaken to pieces. By going as fast as one can safely drive, the wheels hit only the tops of the ridges. Charles had never heard of such a thing in California, but after several bone-jarring miles he was ready to follow my advice and to his amazement found that it worked.

Back in the Park Hotel in Teheran, after showering off the desert dust we called Mr. Entezam to learn whether the Pir had returned. As only three days remained before our return flight to New York, we were anxious because the purpose of our trip was really to meet a holy man recommended by our former Group Leader in Washington. The next morning we set out with Mr. Entezam in one of those small Teheran taxis that swerve recklessly around obstacles in the streets, be they people, cars, or animals. The best thing the passenger can do is to hold tightly to whatever one can grasp and pray. The Pir's Khaneghah ("place of dervishes") was in Shahr Ray, an ancient suburb of Teheran. The way passes through South Teheran with its congested streets and unbelievable poverty and slums, some little more than caves dug into embankments along the road.

The taxi slowed as we approached a rather large walled compound with a small door near the end of it. Mr. Entezam rang, and when the gate opened we entered a garden with flowers and fruit trees and a gardener's shed near the back. We were ushered to chairs and a small table near a pool and asked to wait. In a short time we were motioned to come to the house. We went up eight or ten steps to the porch where we saw several pairs of shoes and realized we should remove ours, which we added to the collection. We went on into a room where a thin gray-haired man, Pir Maleknia Naseralishah, was seated on a cot. I noticed that unlike the Sheikh in Isfahan he was wearing Western dress, but what really held me were his eyes. I couldn't decide whether they were brown or hazel or gray with light flecks in them. They were so compelling, his gaze so direct but calm, that I could not look at his face for more than a few seconds. Otherwise I felt somehow content to be there. During our entire visit, which lasted perhaps half or three-quarters of an hour, I was alternately glad to be there, and then, looking into his eyes again, was terrified. There was so much force there, something not of this world, as if for all that frail and delicate body, the power behind those eyes could shatter a mountain. When we got up to go he rose and followed us to the door. Looking directly at me, he said, "Khanum (the lady) is afraid I will steal her heart!" I was surely afraid of something, and at the same time very reluctant to leave. The feeling, however, didn't keep us from returning to New York. We were like that—uptight wasps who kept to their schedules even if they didn't want to. So the next day we took our flight to New York, both wanting to remain in Iran.

Life went on about as it always had except that my health began to fail. Although I was already on a strict low fat diet, I began to have frequent attacks of severe gastrointestinal pain. I continued going to the Gurdjieff Foundation and to Armonk, where I was leading the weaving project. I would be felled by the severe attacks of pain and nausea, but after a day or two of rest I could resume my activities. Two years passed this way, and we came to the end of another season of the Work. During this time my status in the Gurdjieff Work became steadily more distressing. Charles had been leading a small group of young people under Mrs. Welch's aegis, and I had been sitting in on these meetings as well. One day she told Charles that he should meet with his group in her apartment along with a man from our own group, but she did not invite me. I got the message. I was not wanted. This was only one of many little slights I suffered from her over the years. Other women in our group had suffered similar slights from Mrs. Welch as well. At the same time, as I write this, I must add that I shall be forever grateful to her husband, Dr. Welch, for the help and comfort he gave me in relieving my attacks of pain and nausea. The Welches lived above us, and because my regular physician who lived downtown refused to make house calls, Dr. Welch's professional care was a godsend.

Finally on the weekend before the closing at Armonk in 1968 for the summer the final humiliation dropped on me. On arrival we were to check the bulletin board to learn what the assignments were for the session. We arrived in time for breakfast. As we passed the bulletin board on the way to the dining room I saw everyone's name on the list except the wife of one of the members of Group I and mine. I thought at first this was a mistake and so did Charles. He asked someone and was told it was no mistake. I sat down at breakfast and began to cry. I couldn't stop. I will never forget the reaction of a man who had been in the Work as long as we had, an editor for one of the major book publishers. He had no idea why I was crying, but he had never seen me in such a state and he became very upset. After breakfast Mrs. Welch, our group leader, called Charles and me into a small sitting room near the dining room, and thinking I was crying about my mother, who had died a few weeks before, she told me to go ahead and cry. It infuriated me that she should have so little awareness as not to know what was the matter. She had helped make the list on which my name was missing. It emerged that the point of the weekend was to designate people at our level in the Work who were to become Group Leaders and to meet with members of Group I to discuss what it meant to be a Group Leader and what the responsibility involved. I was not to be among them. So this was the end and aim of our years of effort? To make matters worse, a few young people from outside New York City who had been in the Work for only two or three years were invited.

The whole thing appalled us. In fact Charles couldn't believe it at first. He thought some sort of joke was being played on him. He knew he didn't have what it took to be what he thought a Group Leader should be. But we quickly realized that it was no joke, and that, moreover, there was no secret teaching. There was no further spiritual development possible in the Work. They had not given us what we wanted because they didn't have it themselves. If you have ever experienced even for a few days that feeling of the bottom dropping out from under you after years of time, effort and hope, you know what we were experiencing. It seems to me now that for a short time we were in an intellectual and emotional void like shock. This was exactly the right state to be in for what happened next week when we returned to the city in June 1968.

One of the regularly scheduled events at the Gurdjieff Foundation was the Tuesday evening reading in the large movement hall. One of the Group I members or a long-time Gurdjieffian would read for about 20 minutes from one of the writings of Gurdjieff or Ouspensky, followed by questions and answers. As I was dressing to go to the reading, I was seized with an urge to wear a coat I had bought on our first trip to Iran. It was a handsome garment of light wool three-quarter sleeveless coat entirely embroidered in green, red, blue and white geometric shapes. The fabric was a product of the tribes in the desert bordering on Pakistan. I had not worn it, nor thought about it, until that night.

I arrived a little later than usual. No chairs were available in the rows in the center of the hall before the portable stage where the readers sat, so I quietly moved on around the hall to find vacant chairs on the side. As I sat down I saw Charles settled in the central section. I began to have a feeling I couldn't identify. The reader began, and I listened as well as I could, trying to ignore what was happening to me. By the time the reading was finished a great longing like homesickness rose up in me. When the questions were finished and people were leaving their places there was no mistake about what I was feeling; it was a longing to go back to Iran. I glanced at my watch and it was just seven o'clock. I started for the foyer and pushed my way toward Charles, who turned to me and said, "Did anything happen to you in there?" I replied, "Yes, we must go to Iran. We've been called." He said, "Exactly! It was so strong I looked at my watch. It was seven o'clock."

What were hoping to find in Iran? Answer: a flight from the Gurdjieff work and with whatever hope there was left to find a way that offered the means or method of real spiritual development to give us a clue to what life is all about. Did we find it? Yes, but we didn't succeed in attaining it. We had been troubled by the humiliation I had encountered at Armonk, and we were having real doubts about whether the Gurdjieff Work would take us where we wanted to go. So a few days later we made reservations for Teheran. When we arrived on August 1st, 1968 we discovered that Pir Naseralishah (or Hazrat Agha, as his dervishes call him) had just returned from Europe, but he wanted to see us.

When we entered Hazrat Agha's room at the Khaneghah in Shahr Ray we both said: "You called us!" He smiled and replied: "I've been calling you for two years. Your hearing is very bad!" After meeting with him several times, imploring him for help, he finally initiated us into his order on August 18th. On our flight to New York on the following day we realized that something momentous had happened to us. In the state I was in I had no doubt that God was alive and well.

We broke our flight by a stopover in Amsterdam. After we had settled into the hotel we decided to take a walk. As we strolled along in the warm summer evening we heard male voices and a group of young men came around the corner toward us. Two of them were young men who had been in the Gurdjieff group my husband had been leading in New York. Recognition was instantaneous, and they stopped dead. We were equally stunned by the coincidence, for we supposed they were traveling in Russia. One of them remarked recently that though it happened years ago, this was still the most astounding event of his life.

During one of our visits after our initiation I was traumatized by an experience that colored the rest of my days as a dervish. We were sitting with Hazrat Agha in his small room in the Khaneghah in Teheran one evening when without explanation he suddenly rose and left Charles and me alone, evidently to join some dervishes in another room whom I never saw. Shortly his brother came and motioned to Charles to come with him. They went to another part of the Khaneghah, and I sat there alone—and sat, and sat! I began to cry. When Hazrat Agha's brother saw me he quickly found Charles and brought him back to me. All I could say between the flood of tears was: "I want to leave. I want to go back to the hotel."

Hazrat Agha returned and said: "Don't leave." He implied that it was not a good thing to disobey him by going when he had told me to stay. He said something to Charles, who told me Hazrat Agha had said I should stay. I got the message clearly that to leave would hinder my spiritual growth, but I just couldn't stay, and Charles took me away. I ask myself today if it is true that I cut myself off from significant help when I failed this first test of obedience.

Agha could be hard and he was hard on both of us. A couple of years later when we met him in Zurich and went on with him to Hamburg he alternately castigated us for character defects and suggested impossible and unimaginable changes in our living arrangements. I was the focus of his severity but Charles was translating, and Agha warned him that if he took my part in the exchange it would be very bad. This went on for several days and drove us to the brink of suicide. Nevertheless for years we continued to do what we thought Agha expected of us, still hoping to find the love and affirmation that had appeared so attractive in our early encounters with him. Whatever the esoteric intention of this abrupt shift from kindness to harshness, it was lost on two Americans. Gradually I began to see that this was a repetition of the cycles of hope and disappointment that had afflicted my entire life. Naturally, I ultimately withdrew my hope.

Epilogue

My life with its many ups and downs has been so helpful to my understanding of the world that I cannot be dissatisfied. It has offered me so many choices—so many possibilities. At nearly 90 I could say my life has done a job on me. My mother pushed me out of that miserable little hamlet in which I was born, the only viable solution she could see for the future of her teenage daughter. If she had done nothing other than this to launch me into the adult world I would forgive her for all her lapses as a mother, for all the years of mismanagement and painful neglect.

Now I see the numbing conditions of my childhood from a vastly different perspective. It has been a painful journey to find my identity and to stop acting to substantiate it, to fortify it, and to convince others and myself that I have the right to be here. I no longer have the "love-hoped-for" ache. When I bring up the memory of my parents I see them as small and vulnerable, playing out their lives in that pinched off little spot stranded in the 19th century. They pursued their affairs with minimal expectations unaware of the changes that had come to that part of the world with the 20th century. They gave it all they had, each with his or her assets and limitations, to achieve a considerable success, given their circumstances. With my transformed perception of them my impulse is to protect them. I want to tell them it wasn't the way they thought. But how could I have told them then, when I didn't know either? How strange that we don't come here prepared for our life and with the wisdom to deal with it. "Love hoped for" has been a long grieving.

In spite of my disappointing experience with Sufism, I have no doubt that Hazrat Agha was one of the greatest, if not the greatest teacher of our times. I am grateful to him for showing me flaws in my character that had been hidden from me, but above all, paradoxically, he gave me an unshakeable faith in God.

Now "hope" has been retired, leaving love standing triumphant over those little graves of hurts and emotional scars of childhood. Love is no longer hoped for, it is found. It is close to impossible to explain a miraculous transformation. I have left flickering uncertainty, doubt and fear behind. Certainly the effort of recalling and recording this account had much to do with it. I had worked on the first part of this memoir twenty years ago, yet only in the past year has my view of my early life and myself profoundly changed.

Life may hand you a big surprise after you think you have exhausted all possible ways to self-knowledge or transformation. I had heard over the years various favorable and some almost miraculous accounts of "Hands On Healing," but I had never met a healer. It was therefore with only mild interest that I went with my husband and a few friends to what I had understood to be a demonstration of this method. Soon after the leader of the demonstration began to speak I discovered it wasn't about what I understood "Hands On Healing" to be. It was instead something called Energetic Healing. After she finished her introduction she asked for a volunteer to demonstrate her practice. By that time I was so interested and so attracted (though by what I could not say) I was sure I wanted to volunteer. This was something I had never done in my life. Wanting to be chosen I made a spectacle of myself by frantically waving my up-raised hand. She looked around the room and after what felt like an eternity asked me to get onto the table. I have had my quota of ailments and illnesses—most recently an irregularity in my heart function. She began her work by passing a hand raised a few inches over my head down the length of my torso, never touching my body. She announced that one hip was higher than the other and that she sensed digestive problems, both of which were true. Returning to the area of the heart she stopped and said she wouldn't touch that area. She said there was some difficulty there and she wasn't going to work on that in a demonstration.

This was my introduction to Martha Piesco Hoff. Since that Saturday in 2002 I have received much help and knowledge from her, not all confined to the functioning of the body. Questions, problems with my family, painful memories that have tormented me for years are now transformed into an entirely different interpretation of my relationship to them. As I have written the last part of this memoir I have experienced moments of incredibly intense feeling, grief, tears, sadness, and regret. A vivid recall of the past has penetrated my flesh and bones. I have no doubt this transformation would not have occurred without my energetic healing work with Martha.

I must also express my gratitude to my parents for giving me a good body and a mind that enabled me to detect, unravel, and act on difficult situations that broadened me and improved my character. Above and beyond all I cannot adequately express my gratitude to God for His strength and guidance without which none of this would have been possible.

0-595-33407-5